Gregor Koenig

An EEG-based Model of Daytime Vigilance Trends

Gregor Koenig

An EEG-based Model of Daytime Vigilance Trends

Südwestdeutscher Verlag für Hochschulschriften

Impressum / Imprint
Bibliografische Information der Deutschen Nationalbibliothek: Die Deutsche Nationalbibliothek verzeichnet diese Publikation in der Deutschen Nationalbibliografie; detaillierte bibliografische Daten sind im Internet über http://dnb.d-nb.de abrufbar.
Alle in diesem Buch genannten Marken und Produktnamen unterliegen warenzeichen-, marken- oder patentrechtlichem Schutz bzw. sind Warenzeichen oder eingetragene Warenzeichen der jeweiligen Inhaber. Die Wiedergabe von Marken, Produktnamen, Gebrauchsnamen, Handelsnamen, Warenbezeichnungen u.s.w. in diesem Werk berechtigt auch ohne besondere Kennzeichnung nicht zu der Annahme, dass solche Namen im Sinne der Warenzeichen- und Markenschutzgesetzgebung als frei zu betrachten wären und daher von jedermann benutzt werden dürften.

Bibliographic information published by the Deutsche Nationalbibliothek: The Deutsche Nationalbibliothek lists this publication in the Deutsche Nationalbibliografie; detailed bibliographic data are available in the Internet at http://dnb.d-nb.de.
Any brand names and product names mentioned in this book are subject to trademark, brand or patent protection and are trademarks or registered trademarks of their respective holders. The use of brand names, product names, common names, trade names, product descriptions etc. even without a particular marking in this work is in no way to be construed to mean that such names may be regarded as unrestricted in respect of trademark and brand protection legislation and could thus be used by anyone.

Coverbild / Cover image: www.ingimage.com

Verlag / Publisher:
Südwestdeutscher Verlag für Hochschulschriften
ist ein Imprint der / is a trademark of
OmniScriptum GmbH & Co. KG
Heinrich-Böcking-Str. 6-8, 66121 Saarbrücken, Deutschland / Germany
Email: info@svh-verlag.de

Herstellung: siehe letzte Seite /
Printed at: see last page
ISBN: 978-3-8381-5084-0

Zugl. / Approved by: Wien, Medical University of Vienna, 2012

Copyright © 2015 OmniScriptum GmbH & Co. KG
Alle Rechte vorbehalten. / All rights reserved. Saarbrücken 2015

Für meine Eltern.

Abstract

The objective quantification of vigilance and sleepiness is more than ever an important focus in research. Impaired daytime vigilance due to insufficient sleep and low sleep quality has become an inevitable fact in industrialized countries. The reasons are manifold, the consequences may be fatal. Studies show that the the loss of human life but also the economic costs are substantial.

The aim of this thesis is to objectively describe long-term daytime vigilance and sleepiness based on Electroencephalogram (EEG)-derived variables.

The homeostatic and circadian influences on daytime vigilance and sleepiness are well known. Borbély describes them in the two process model of sleep regulation. This thesis provides empirical evidence for these processes based on objective EEG-based variables. Such variables can be used in a model describing and predicting diurnal vigilance and sleepiness and to separate EEG data from subjects after sleep-deprivation from data after normal sleep. It is further shown that the vigilance trends of several variables can be used to classify daytime EEG data under sleep deprivation and after normal sleep.

An exploratory study was conducted under real-world conditions, including 26 healthy female and male subjects. For two 24 hour periods we recorded EEG channels using a mobile system, along with hourly subjective sleepiness ratings and reaction times. The sessions consisted of a night and a day under a sleep-deprived and a normal-sleep condition. The two sessions were embedded in 14 days of recording actigraphy and sleep quality ratings.

52 EEG-based variables were derived from the acquired data, such as frequency band powers, band ratios, complexity and entropy measures, and EEG events such as alpha events or diurnal sleep spindles. EEG artifacts are also used as variables.

The actigraphy data was used to estimate the individual circadian rhythm. For the analysis of circadian trends we scaled the data relative to the individual circadian phase, for the homeostatic analysis relative to the time of wake up.

Using statistical means such as correlation coefficients and paired t-tests we analyzed the variables' homeostatic and circadian trends, compared them to the two-process model, and tested the variables' ability to distinguish between the data under sleep deprivation and data after normal sleep. Based on the homeostatic trends of a combination of variables a model was build that is able classify EEG data according to the two conditions. The correctness was assessed by a k-fold cross-validation and the significance was tested based on a χ^2 test.

In the analysis several variables were discovered that show behavior significantly correlated to the two-process model. Especially the daytime-trends of EEG-artifacts provide an interesting insight, for instance the artifacts caused by eye movements correlate negatively with the homeostatic timescale. The standard deviation of the theta band is an examples for a variable with a strong circadian behavior.

Several variables are able to separate sleep-deprived data from data after normal sleep. Good examples for separating variables are the relative delta-band power or the $(\theta+\alpha)/\beta$ ratio. These variables can serve as descriptive and predictive biomarkers for diurnal vigilance and sleepiness in the EEG during daytime.

The homeostatic trends of a combination of variables were used as a classification model and showed significantly correct classification rates of 80 %. The best performing variables were based on EEG activity in the theta-, very high beta-, and delta-frequency-bands as well as variables derived from eye and muscle artifacts.

We were able to provide significant empirical evidence for the circadian and homeostatic behavior of EEG-based variables.

Our exploratory work is an important step towards objectively describing and predicting daytime vigilance and sleepiness. The positive results contribute to a better understanding of the representation of attentive processes in the EEG and encourage us to investigate the topic on a larger scale.

Kurzfassung

Die objektive Quantifizierung von Vigilanz und Schläfrigkeit ist mehr denn je ein wichtiger Forschungsgegenstand. Besonders in Industrieländern leiden Menschen unter unzureichendem Schlaf und einer niedrigen Schlafqualität, was zu eingeschränkter Tagesvigilanz führt. Die Gründe dafür sind mannigfaltig, die Konsequenzen können tödlich sein. Studien zeigen, dass auch die volkswirtschaftlichen Folgekosten enorm sind.

Das Ziel dieser Dissertation ist die objektive Beschreibung von Tagesvigilanz und Tagesschläfrigkeit im gesamten Tagesverlauf auf der Basis von Elektroenzephalogramm (EEG)-basierten Variablen.

Dass die Tagesvigilanz und Schläfrigkeit von homöostatischen und zirkadianen Prozessen beeinflusst wird, ist aus der Literatur bekannt. Borbély beschreibt die beiden Prozesse im Zwei-Prozess Modell zur Schlafregulation. Diese Dissertation belegt diese Prozesse empirisch mit objektiven EEG-basierten Variablen. Solche Variablen können in einem Modell zur Beschreibung und Vorhersage von Tagesvigilanz und Schläfrigkeit verwendet werden. Auch die Separierung von EEG-Daten von Personen unter Schlafentzug von Daten nach normallangem Schlaf ist mit den EEG-basierten Variablen möglich. Darüber hinaus zeigt diese Arbeit, dass es mit Hilfe von einigen dieser Variablen möglich ist EEG-Daten in 'Schlafentzug' und 'normaler Schlaf' zu klassifizieren.

Im Rahmen der Dissertation wurde eine Studie unter realistischen Bedingungen durchgeführt. Dafür wurden EEG-Signale sowie stündliche subjektive Schläfrigkeitseinschätzungen und Reaktionszeiten von 26 gesunden männlichen und weiblichen Personen für zweimal 24 Stunden aufgezeichnet. Die Aufzeichnungseinheiten bestanden jeweils aus einer Nacht und einem Tag. Bei einer der beiden Einheiten wurde Schlafentzug induziert. Die beiden Einheiten waren in einem 14-tägigen Überwachungszeitraum eingebettet, in dem ein Aktivitätsprofil (Aktigramm) und ein Schlaftagebuch aufgezeichnet wurden.

Von den aufgezeichneten Daten wurden 52 EEG-basierte Variablen abgeleitet, wie zum Beispiel die Power von EEG Frequenzbändern, Quotienten aus Frequenzbändern, Komplexitäts- und Entropiemaße sowie Variablen, basierend auf EEG-Ereignissen und EEG-Artefakten.

Mit statistischen Mitteln wie Korrelationskoeffizienten und einem paarweisen t-Test wurden die homöostatischen und zirkadianen Trends in den Daten analysiert und mit dem Zwei-Prozess-Modell verglichen. Weiters wurden die Variablen auf Ihre Eignung untersucht, wie gut sie EEG-Daten unter Schlafentzug von Daten nach Normalschlaf unterscheiden können.

Basierend auf der Kombination der homöostatischen Trends von Variablen wurde ein Klassifizierungsmodell erstellt. Die Korrektheit der Klassifizierung wurde mit Hilfe eines k-fachen Kreuzvalidierungsverfahrens überprüft und die Signifikanz mit einem χ^2 Test erhoben.

Die Analyse der Daten zeigt, dass einige Variablen ein Verhalten aufweisen, das signifikant mit dem Zwei-Prozess Modell korreliert. Dabei wurden Trends bei Artefakt-basierten Variablen festgestellt, zum Beispiel ein starker negativer homöostatischer Trend bei durch Augenbewegungen verursachten Artefakten. Die Standardabweichung der Aktivität im Theta-Frequenz-Band ist ein Beispiel für einen starken zirkadianen Trend.

Einige Variablen zeigen eine gute Eignung zur Trennung von EEG-Daten unter Schlafentzug von Daten nach normalem Schlaf, zum Beispiel die Power des relativen Delta-Bands oder der $(\theta + \alpha)/\beta$ Quotient. Diese Variablen können als beschreibende oder vorhersagende Biomarker für Tagesvigilanz und Tagesschläfrigkeit verwendet werden.

Die homöostatischen Trends einer Kombination von Variablen wurden als Klassifikationsmodell verwendet und zeigten einen signifikanten Anteil von 80 % korrekten Klassifizierungen. Die am besten geeignetsten Variablen basierten auf EEG Aktivität im Theta-, sehr hohen Beta- und Delta-Frequenz-Band sowie Variablen, die auf Augen- und Muskel-Artefakten beruhen.

Wir konnten signifikante empirische Hinweise für homöostatisches und zirkadianes Verhalten von EEG-basierten Variablen geben.

Diese Arbeit ist ein wichtiger Schritt in Richtung einer objektiven Beschreibung und Vorhersage von Vigilanz und Schläfrigkeit. Die erfolgreichen Resultate tragen zu einem besseren Verständnis der Abbildung von Aufmerksamkeitsprozessen im EEG bei und ermutigen uns das Thema weiter zu verfolgen.

Acknowledgments

First of all I want to thank my thesis supervisor Professor Georg Dorffner for the numerous meetings and profound discussions during the last three years. His guidance and support was essential on the path to successfully finish this thesis.
I also want to thank Professor Josef Zeitlhofer for his support during the last years and his valuable reflections from the neurological and clinical perspective, as well as Professor Winfried Mayr for his contributions in our thesis committee meetings.

I want to thank Siegfried Wassertheurer and Manfred Bammer from the AIT Austrian Institute of Technology GmbH for giving me the chance to work on this thesis for more than three years and for providing me a stimulating working environment.
I also want to thank all my colleagues at AIT for their generous support, especially Sten Hanke, Christopher Mayer, Bernhard Hametner, Xenia Descovich, and Martin Bachler. Thank you for so many fruitful discussions and reflections.

I want to thank the team of the Siesta Group for giving me support during the conduction of the study and the data handling, especially Erna Loretz and Georg Gruber.
Gerhard Klösch from the Department of Neurology at the Vienna General Hospital supported me especially during the study, I want to thank him for his help and many interesting discussions.

During the last three years I could always count on the support of my family and friends. I want to thank my parents Irmgard and Josef for encouraging me in my decision to write this thesis and for supporting me in any situation.
Finally I want to thank all my friends who helped my through the completion of this thesis and who provided the necessary balance to my working life.
Merci surtout à Guy-Didier Debast pour ses encouragements et le partage de moments de détente si précieux pendant cette longue période d'écriture.

Gregor Koenig

This research was accomplished within the context of the following projects:

- ARCCore, initiated by the AIT Austrian Institute of Technology GmbH, Health and Environment Department, Biomedical Systems, and is funded by the AIT Austrian Institute of Technology GmbH, the government of Lower Austria, and the European Regional Development Fund (ERDF).
- KlaVig - Klassifizierung von Vigilanzstadien basierend auf EOG und EEG, funded by the Austrian Research Promotion Agency (FFG).

Contents

Abstract	V

1 Introduction   1

1.1	Motivation	1
1.2	Aim of the Thesis	4
1.3	Why an EEG-based Approach?	5
1.4	Outline	7

2 Electrical Brain Activity   9

2.1	Introduction to Biosignals			9
2.2	Origin of Electrical Brain Activity			11
	2.2.1	Neurophysiology		11
		2.2.1.1	Neurons	11
		2.2.1.2	Neuroanatomy	15
		2.2.1.3	Cortical Organization of Neurons	15
		2.2.1.4	Electrical Properties of Pyramidal Cells	16
2.3	Measurement of Electrical Brain Activity			17
	2.3.1	Invasive Recording of Electrical Activity		18

XI

		2.3.1.1	Intra-cortical Electrodes	18
		2.3.1.2	Electrocorticogram	18
	2.3.2	Electroencephalography		19
		2.3.2.1	EEG Recording	20
2.4	Analysis of EEG Signals			25
	2.4.1	EEG Artifacts		25
		2.4.1.1	Physiological EEG Artifacts	25
		2.4.1.2	Environmental EEG Artifacts	28
	2.4.2	Analysis of Frequencies		29
		2.4.2.1	Time Domain and Frequency Domain	29
		2.4.2.2	EEG Frequency Bands	30
		2.4.2.3	Power Spectral Density	32
	2.4.3	Filtering		32
	2.4.4	Analysis in the Time Domain		33
		2.4.4.1	Arithmetic Mean	33
		2.4.4.2	Median and Quantiles	33
		2.4.4.3	Standard Deviation	34
		2.4.4.4	Skewness	34
		2.4.4.5	Kurtosis	35
	2.4.5	Complexity Measures		35
		2.4.5.1	Permutation Entropy Index	36
2.5	Applications of the EEG			38
	2.5.1	Epilepsy		38

		2.5.2	LORETA	38

	2.5.3	Brain Computer Interfaces	41
		2.5.3.1 Focused Attention	42
		2.5.3.2 Motor Imagery	43
	2.5.4	Anesthesia	44
	2.5.5	Sleep Medicine	44
	2.5.6	Other Applications	44
		2.5.6.1 Brain Death	44
		2.5.6.2 Localization of Brain Lesions	44
		2.5.6.3 Testing Afferent Pathways	45
		2.5.6.4 Biofeedback	45

3 Attention, Vigilance, and Sleepiness — 47

3.1	Introduction	47
3.2	Definitions and Physiological Basics	48
	3.2.1 Consciousness and Attention	48
	3.2.1.1 Consciousness	48
	3.2.1.2 Attention	49
	3.2.2 Vigilance	50
	3.2.2.1 Alertness	50
	3.2.3 Sleepiness and Fatigue	50
3.3	Models and Processes of Sleepiness and Alertness	52
	3.3.1 Measuring the Circadian Rhythm	53

3.3.2 Estimating the Circadian Rhythm using Actigraphy 55

3.4 Quantification of Vigilance 58

    3.4.1 Subjective Quantification 58

        3.4.1.1 Karolinska Sleepiness Scale 58

        3.4.1.2 Epworth Sleepiness Scale 59

        3.4.1.3 Stanford Sleepiness Scale 60

    3.4.2 Quantification of Behavior 60

        3.4.2.1 Reaction-Time and Vigilance Tests 60

        3.4.2.2 Psychomotor Vigilance Test 61

        3.4.2.3 Multiple Sleep Latency and Maintenance of Wakefulness Tests 62

        3.4.2.4 Video Analysis 63

        3.4.2.5 Special Environments - Vehicle Parameters 63

    3.4.3 Physiological Quantification 64

        3.4.3.1 Electroencephalogram 64

        3.4.3.2 Electrooculogram, Blinks, and Pupils 80

        3.4.3.3 Heart Rate 82

        3.4.3.4 Electromyogram 83

4 Methods   **85**

4.1 An Exploratory Study 86

    4.1.1 Design 86

    4.1.2 Time Schedule 87

    4.1.3 Subjects 90

	4.1.4	Actigraphy	91
	4.1.5	KSS	91
	4.1.6	Reaction Time Test	92
	4.1.7	Sleep Diary	93
	4.1.8	Log-Book	94
	4.1.9	Biosignal Recording	94
	4.1.10	Ethical Consideration	96
	4.1.11	Data Security and Subject Privacy	96
	4.1.12	Risk-Benefit Analysis	96
4.2	EEG Artifact Handling		98
	4.2.1	Artifact-based Variables	101
4.3	EEG-based Variables		102
	4.3.1	Frequency-band-based Variables	102
	4.3.2	Amplitude-based Variables	103
	4.3.3	Complexity-based Variables	104
	4.3.4	Event-based Variables	104
	4.3.5	Spectral Variables	106
4.4	Analysis of the Data		107
4.5	Validation Strategies		111
	4.5.1	Homeostatic Properties	111
	4.5.2	Circadian Properties	112
	4.5.3	Trends following the 3-Process Model	114
	4.5.4	Separation of the two Conditions	115

		4.5.5	Classification of Daytime Trends	115

5 Results 119

- 5.1 Subjects . . . 119
  - 5.1.1 Data Quality . . . 120
- 5.2 Homeostatic Trends . . . 123
- 5.3 Circadian Trends . . . 128
- 5.4 Trends Following the 3-Process Model . . . 132
- 5.5 Separability . . . 135
- 5.6 Model-based Classification . . . 138

6 Discussion 143

- 6.1 Homeostatic Trends . . . 144
- 6.2 Circadian trends . . . 146
- 6.3 Model of Alertness and Sleepiness . . . 147
- 6.4 Separability . . . 148
- 6.5 Model-based Classification . . . 149
- 6.6 Future Research . . . 151
  - 6.6.1 Multi Modal Approach . . . 151
  - 6.6.2 Additional Variables . . . 151
  - 6.6.3 Improve Classification . . . 152
  - 6.6.4 Additional Evaluation . . . 152

A Study Documents 153

Nomenclature	**162**
List of Figures	**165**
List of Tables	**167**
Bibliography	**185**
About the Author	**187**

Chapter 1

Introduction

1.1 Motivation

The objective quantification of vigilance and sleepiness is more than ever an important focus in research. Impaired daytime vigilance due to insufficient sleep and low sleep quality has become an inevitable fact in industrialized countries.

The reasons are manifold and range from life style and insufficient sleep hygiene up to sleep disorders.
Research groups such as the team around Prof. Åkerstedt at the Karolinska Institutet in Sweden have analyzed the topic with a focus on work environments [9]. A wide range of work environments exists that include monotonous tasks, which require constant concentration and alertness. Examples are the environments of air traffic controllers [28], truck or train drivers [160], and controllers of power plants. Irregular work shifts and working hours aggravate the situation.
Stress is another major factor related to reduced sleep quality and even to insomnia [14]. A large number of persons in industrialized countries are affected by stress and have to cope with the possible consequences. The burnout syndrome is also known to influence sleep quality in a negative way [102].
Patients suffering from sleep disorders are also another group of individuals with reduced sleep quality. Disturbed sleep can have a wide range of clinical reasons such as obstructive sleep apnea, the restless leg syndrome, or side-effects resulting from medication.
Drugs and medication also play an important role in influencing sleep quality and daytime

vigilance. This effects can either be the original intention of the drug or may appear as unwanted side-effects.

Insufficient sleep and low sleep quality lead to impaired daytime vigilance and sleepiness [49]. The consequences may be fatal. Studies about road safety show that up to 30 % of fatal road accidents are related to sleepiness [109]. The loss of human life but also the economic costs are substantial.

Besides these direct concerns in public safety and public health a wide range of conditions and illnesses are known to be influenced by sleep and sleep quality. Besides a lowered life quality in general it is associated with metabolic issues such as diabetes, obesity, and the metabolic syndrome [71].

Åkerstedt et al. [10] also show the relationship of disturbed sleep to accidents and long-term health.

In the clinical practice a broad range of methods is employed to estimate daytime vigilance and sleepiness. One example are subjective sleepiness ratings on standardized scales such as the Karolinska Sleepiness Scale (KSS) or the Epworth Sleepiness Scale (ESS)[56].

An indirect approach to quantify sleepiness is the measurement of the reaction time. It is claimed that sleepiness and concentration can be measured using monotonous reaction time tests such as the Macworth clock-test [96].

Another approach to quantify the phenomenon is the measurement of the time it takes a person to fall asleep. The Multiple Sleep Latency Test (MSLT) [56] requires a special laboratory environment and is very time consuming and cost intensive. This test is seen as the current standard for quantifying daytime sleepiness. The tendency to fall asleep and the ability to stay awake are two distinct physiological processes [134]. Whereas the first phenomenon is measured by the MSLT the second is quantified by the Maintenance of Wakefulness Test (MWT) and the Oxford Sleep Resistance Test (OSLER), which is a simplified version the the MWT[56].

Besides these test protocols the transition from wakefulness to sleep is also indicated by several physiological parameters [111]. Actigraphy is the recording of body movements [157]. It can be used as a rough value for alertness and is used to detect sleep-wake cycles and circadian rhythms.

Pupillometry [104] uses the size and variability of the human pupil as a physiological parameter. Several observations concerning the eyes such as the blink rate or slow lateral eye movements [45] are known to correlate with the sleepiness. The recording of the

1.1 Motivation

movement of the eyes is also known as electrooculography (EOG) [32, 52].

Respiration, peripheral and core body temperature, or the skin potential [111] are some other physiological variables that may indicate changes in daytime vigilance.

The electroencephalogram (EEG) is used by many groups to measure daytime vigilance and sleepiness [38, 91, 123]. It is seen as the gold standard of vigilance measurement by some authors. Most authors analyze the frequency content and amplitude behavior of the EEG. Some research groups try to classify stages of wakefulness [93] based on the EEG. An example for a descriptive stage-based approach are the COMSTAT rules [146]. Several research groups [45, 122] propose multi-modal approaches that combine the EEG and EOG.

Up to now, no standardized and established method of objectively quantifying daytime vigilance and sleepiness under real-world conditions exists.

1.2 Aim of the Thesis

The aim of this thesis is to objectively describe long-term daytime vigilance and sleepiness based on EEG-derived variables. This can be achieved by finding empirically validated electro-physiological biomarkers in the EEG, which can serve as the basis for a model of daytime vigilance trends.

A long-term trend gives a more complete and detailed picture about daytime vigilance compared to other ways of vigilance quantification that are focused on short-term measurement. The results of this thesis shall have validity in real-world environments as well as in the clinical context.

The first step is an assessment of the state of the art in the field, which is essential to generate new ideas and to be able to use the successful and promising approaches documented by other authors as the basis for the project.

To empirically test and verify the ideas and approaches a specific exploratory study shall be designed, where biosignals are recorded under conditions that induced the necessary variability of sleepiness and vigilance, for instance sleep deprivation. The data shall be recorded with a mobile device in a real-world environment.

Besides the biosignals the study protocol shall be designed in a way that provides a range of additional indicators of vigilance, for instance actigraphy, reaction time tests, and subjective sleepiness ratings. These additional indicators are valuable in the validation of the variables based on biosignals, for instance the individual circadian rhythm [73], sleep debt, or sleep pressure [126].

Because of the mobile recording system the artifact detection and handling is of crucial importance. Models of the diurnal trends of vigilance shall be built based on the properly processed data. Those models that show significant diurnal trends which make it possible to separate sleep deprived data from normal data can further serve as the basis of a model for the classification of EEG-data.

1.3 Why an EEG-based Approach?

In this project the EEG was chosen as the main physiological parameter. There are several reasons why the EEG was chosen as the central biosignal for the objective quantification of daytime vigilance.

EEG is an established way to measure electrical brain activity. The non-invasive technology is a standard in clinical practice as well as medical research.

Traditional clinical fields that use the EEG are sleep monitoring, the classification of sleep stages, the monitoring of epilepsy, and the monitoring of patients during and after anesthesia [74, 139, 145]. Sometimes the analysis of the EEG data is still done manually, but information such as sleep stages or the depth of anesthesia can also be extracted automatically from the EEG data [55]. Together with the EOG and the electromyogram (EMG) the EEG is used in the analysis of sleep and sleep stages. Rechtschaffen and Kales [129] defined sleep stages based on these biosignals, which are still used today for analyzing sleep and diagnosing sleep illnesses. The use of the EEG in the measurement of sleep-stages was one reason for the choice.

The survey of state-of-the art literature in the field clearly points out that the EEG holds the necessary information to quantify vigilance directly and objectively. Putilov et al. even regard changes in the spectral analysis of the EEG as the physiological gold standard to identify shifts along the alertness-sleepiness continuum [126]. In literature several approaches exist that try to extract vigilance information out of EEG data [148]. Almost all of these approaches analyze the EEG data in the frequency domain.

Some research groups define stages of vigilance and try to classify the EEG data. This classification is mainly done using automated classifiers, for instance artificial neuronal networks [11]. A flaw of this approach is the definition of the stages. It is very hard to define stages that are physiologically consistent. The main reason is that the underlying physiological processes of vigilance are not yet completely understood.

Several other authors try to find continuous variables of vigilance instead of stages. Such variables can be validated by evaluating the correlation with other measures of vigilance, for instance the alertness-level-index [91]. Some examples of such approaches are distance values [113], the 'brain-rate' [124], or the engagement index [57].

An additional reason why the EEG was chosen as the central biosignal for the research is availability of sophisticated hardware such as wireless sensors and mobile processing units. EEG sensors have evolved massively in recent years and became mobile and wireless [133, 169]. Besides the sensors also the available mobile hardware became more advanced concerning processing capabilities and functionality. This enables the use of more sophisticated techniques in filtering, processing, and analyzing EEG data [148].

For clinical studies this development removes the limiting constraint of measurement under laboratory conditions. A mobile solution enables the monitoring of subjects that move freely in a real-world environment. This leads to more realistic measurements and removes effects such as the first-night-effect, which may be present during polysomnographic monitoring [140, 144]. In the clinical practice mobile EEG devices allow an application outside of laboratory environments. This makes the acquisition of data less time consuming for health-care professionals and allows more specific and realistic measurements.

A drawback of a mobile EEG solution are artifacts. Non-controlled laboratory conditions include many situations that induce technical or physiological artifacts. These influences on the desired biosignal are manageable using modern artifact detection and removal techniques [106, 130, 131].

A property of the EEG as physiological measure is the inter- and intra-subject-variability, which has to be considered when trying to establish generalized models. Pal et al. show that there are feasible ways to deal with these issues [113].

1.4 Outline

This thesis consists of four chapters. This section give a quick overview of the contents of each chapter.

The first chapter is this introduction. The motivation and the aim of the thesis are explained. Several reasons are presented why the EEG was chosen as the basis of the research.

The second chapter discusses electrical brain activity. A profound overview of the physiological basis of the EEG is given. The term 'biosignal' is defined and the origin of electrical activity is explained by describing neurons and the neuro-physiological organization of the brain's cortex. There are several ways to measure the electrical activity of the brain. Several technologies are outlined with a focus on the EEG as a non-invasive example. The manifold options in analyzing the EEG signal are another central topic of this chapter. The necessary preprocessing and several options of EEG signal analysis are explained. The focus lies on those technologies that were used in the course of the research. In the last part of the chapter some important areas where the EEG is applied are presented. This covers applications in clinical practice, such as epilepsy or sleep medicine, but also fields of research such as LORETA and BCI.

In the third chapter several topics concerning attention, vigilance and sleepiness are presented. The chapter begins with a definition of these terms and related notions. This is of special importance as some of the terms have different meanings in different scientific fields. The analysis of the study data presented in the next chapter is inspired and based on the simulation of daytime sleepiness and alertness. Therefore the basics of the simulation and present tools and algorithms are explained that make it possible to estimate the necessary parameters to be able to apply the simulation on real data. Several protocols and methods are used to quantify sleepiness and vigilance in clinical practice such as subjective sleepiness scales and behavior-based options to quantify sleepiness. The focus of this chapter lies on the quantification of vigilance based on physiological variables, especially the EEG. This chapter contains a review of state-of-the-art literature in the field of EEG-based quantification of vigilance and sleepiness.

The fourth chapter covers the practical part of this thesis and documents the research. In the chapter the used methods are introduced. This includes the study design, the study protocol, the choice of subjects and the practical application of technologies such as the actigraphy and reaction time tests. The emphasis lies on the description of EEG recording, on the artifact handling, the EEG-based variables, and the advanced signal processing. The analysis of the data and the followed validation strategies are essential to understand the results.The results are presented in the form of figures and tables and organized in five categories: homeostatic trends of variables, circadian trends, trends following the simulation of daytime sleepiness and alertness, the separability of sleep-deprived from normal daytime EEG-data, and the model-based classification of daytime trends. In the discussion the results are compared to known findings in literature and analyze findings, which were not described before. The final section deals with future research and contains all major ideas that were not covered in the course of this thesis.

In the appendix the documents and forms from the study are presented such as the positive vote of the ethics committee of the Medical University of Vienna or the subjects' informed consent document.
A curriculum vitae of the author is attached at the end of the document.

Chapter 2

Electrical Brain Activity

In this chapter we want to outline the origin, measurement, and analysis of electrical brain activity, with a special focus on the electroencephalogram.

2.1 Introduction to Biosignals

Every organism can be organized in compartments or components that interact in systems. The processes performed by these systems are called physiological processes. As an example the human body consist of several well known systems such as the muscles, the skeleton, the nervous system, or the cardiovascular system. An example of a human physiological process is the signal conduction in the nervous system, which represents a form of communication in the human body [127].

The manifestation of a physiological process is called signal. An example is the nervous system of the human body that uses signals of electrical and chemical nature, such as action potentials and neurotransmitters. During normal operation and during defects or disease of the organism the signals change. With enough insight and understanding of the physiology of the system it becomes possible to observe the signals [127].

Using measurement utilities like electrodes and amplifiers it is possible to objectively quantify, for instance electrical signals. A single measurements results in a scalar value at a time t. Usually it is of interest to monitor a signal over time. The continuous monitoring results in a function of time $x(t)$. Such a continuous recording is also called analogue recording.

For practical reasons concerning digital recording systems it is common to monitor a signal in a discrete way. The values are measured at temporally equidistant instants. $x(n)$ denotes the value of the signal at the discrete instant, or sample, n. The frequency of measuring values is called the sample frequency, which is usually given in samples per second with the unit Hertz. Some authors also use cycles per second (cps), which is synonymous.

A recording system is considered to be digital if the amplitude of each discrete scalar value is represented as a discrete value of a limited scale of possible values.

2.2 Origin of Electrical Brain Activity

An introduction into neurophysiology is essential to understand which electrical potentials an EEG is measuring and where they come from.

2.2.1 Neurophysiology

2.2.1.1 Neurons

Neurons are the smallest entity we describe here. They are the basic building blocks of the nervous system and the generators of the potentials measured by the electrodes of an EEG.

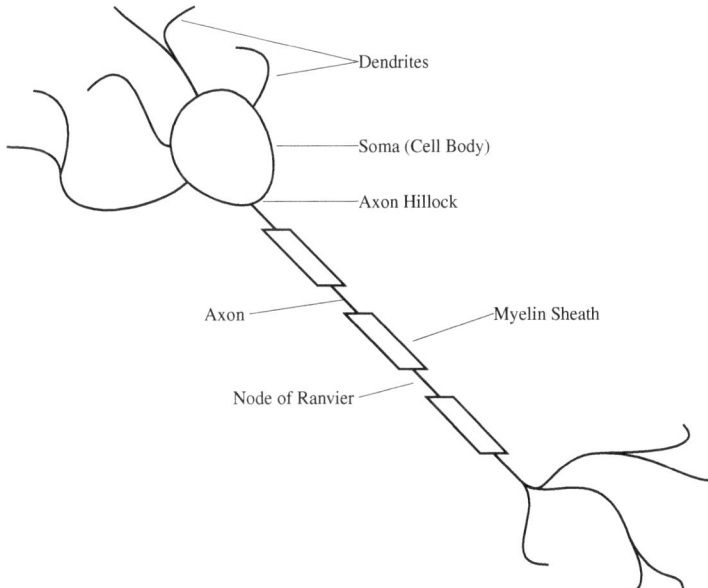

Figure 2.1: A schematic diagram of a typical neuron [51]. The cell body (soma) has several extensions. The usually smaller dentridtes and one longer axon. The axon starts at the axon hillock and can be isolated by a myelin sheath. The gaps in the myelin sheath are called nodes of Ranvier. The end of an axon is called the axon terminal.

2.2.1.1.1 Structure of a Neuron A neuron consists of the cell body, the soma, which usually has two types of extension: the dendrites and the axon. They are depicted schematically in figure 2.1. In most cases the soma has multiple dendrites but only one axon. The axon differs from the dendrites in its size and in the type of branching. An axon can have branches by itself, the collaterals, which might also have branches, called telodentria. The axons can become very long, up to the range of more than a meter. Because of their length they play an important role in bridging long distances in an organism [23].

The dendrites are the parts of the neuron that collect information from other neurons. This happens in an electrochemical way. The information is forwarded to the soma by the dendrites. In the axon the information is forwarded from the soma via the axon to the axon terminal. Via synapses the information is passed on to the dendrites or soma of other neurons. Depending on the neighboring neuron this may have an excitatory or an inhibitory effect. Axons may also pass the information directly to effectors like muscles or glands [23].

The information arrives either directly at the soma or is passed on via the dendrites and gets summed up in the soma. The information is only passed on to the axon if the excitement of the soma surpasses a threshold. The decision whether the action potential is passed on is taken at the beginning of the axon, which is called the axon hog or axon hillock [51]. The axon itself does not alter the information any further and only passes it on.

The neurons in the central nervous system (CNS) differ from the neurons in the peripheral nervous system (PNS) . The CNS consists of the brain and the spinal cord, the PNS of all the other parts of the nervous system. In the PNS the axons and some dendrites can become very long. Some of those long parts of the neuron are covered by an isolating sheath that consists of myelin. The main purpose of this sheath is to improve the speed of the signal conduction in these connecting parts of the neuron. The myelin sheath covering parts of the neuron usually has gaps, which are called nodes of Ranvier. They have a length of about one micrometer [23].

A type of cells that plays an important role for neurons are glia cells. They are distributed all over the nervous system and play different roles. In the CNS they appear as astroglia-, oligodendroglia-, and microglia cells. Astroglia cells are named by their star shaped form and fill the space between neurons and play an important role in the homeostasis of the

2.2 Origin of Electrical Brain Activity 13

ion concentrations in the CNS. Microglia cells are involved in repairing brain damage and rarely appear in healthy tissue. Oligodendroglia cells form the sheath that wraps around axons and long dendrites and forms spiral layers of cell membrane. The isolating sheath of the PNS is formed by Schwann-cells [23].

2.2.1.1.2 Membrane Potentials Cells in general are spaces enclosed by a membrane. Besides cell organelles a cell contains a salty liquid. The ions and organelles move within this cell space and either diffuse or are moved actively. The cell membrane consists of a double layer of lipids. These molecules have a hydrophilic side and a hydrophobic one. In a liquid these molecules form double layers with the hydrophilic layer pointing towards the liquid. For many substances these membranes form an obstacle for free diffusion, especially for ions. This is one of the reasons why membranes have a high electric resistance. Water molecules and substances that are solvable in lipids can easily pass a membrane. The lipids themselves and substances enclosed within the lipid double layer can move freely. Protein molecules are embedded within the lipid layers. They can either be reactive towards the inside or the outside of the cell [23].

Transport proteins play an important role in the exchange of substances between the intracellular and the extracellular space. The transport proteins are pores filled with water and enable ions, for instance K^+ ions, to diffuse.

The concentration of ions differs between the inside and the outside of a cell. Within the cell lots of K^+ ions and only some Na^+ ions are present. In the extracellular space a high concentration of Na^+ ions and Cl^- ions is present. A general rule of physics says that different concentrations of ions in a liquid always tend towards an equilibrium by diffusion. The flow of ions is always proportional to the difference of concentrations, to the border are between the areas, and to the permeability of the border between the concentrations. For example the highly concentrated K^+ ions within a cell can diffuse towards the outside of the cell via the K^+ channels. K^+ ions transport a positive charge to the outside of the cell. This leads to a negatively charged intracellular space, which counteracts the diffusion of the positive ions. At a certain level of negative charge of the interior the diffusion of K^+ ions is stopped. The same amount of K^+ ions enters and leaves the cell via the K^+ channels [50].

The membrane potential can be calculated using the Nerst equation [50]

$$E_{ion} = \frac{RT}{zF} \ln \frac{[Ion]_{out}}{[Ion]_{in}}.$$

R is the ideal gas constant (Joule / Kelvin / mole), T the temperature (Kelvin), z the charge of the ion, F Faraday's constant (Coulombs / mole), and $[Ion]_{out}$ and $[Ion]_{in}$ are the ion concentrations outside and inside the cell.

For a body temperature of $T = 310K$ (= $36.85°C$) and ion concentrations of $[Ion]_{out} = 115 mmol/l$ and $[Ion]_{in} = 4 mmol/l$ the resting membrane potential is

$$E_{ion} = -61mV \, log \, \frac{[Ion]_{out}}{[Ion]_{in}} = -61mV \; x \; 1.59 = -97mV.$$

2.2.1.1.3 Synapses The interconnections between neurons and the connections of neurons with other cell types are called synapses. There are two types of synapses: chemical and electrical synapses.

The majority of synapses are of chemical nature. They typically forward information from a neuron's axon to the next neuron's dendrites. Besides those axo-dentritic connections, there are also axo-somatic, axo-axonal, dendro-dentritic, and somato-somatic synapses. Chemical synapses work according to the following principle: The action potential arrives at the tip of the axon where it leads to the release of neurotransmitters. The neurotransmitters are released from synaptic vesicles into the synaptic cleft, which is the inter-cellular space between the two cells. On the receiving side specific receptors react with the neurotransmitters and ion gates are opened. Depending on the type of neurotransmitter the membrane potential of the receiving cell rises or declines leading to an excitatory post-synaptic potential (EPSP) or an inhibitory post-synaptic potential (IPSP). [23]

The second type of synapse forwards the information between the cells without chemical means. The action potential is forwarded electrically to the next cell, which is connected via a gap junction to the sending cell. This gap junction is formed by connexones, which consist of groups of proteins called connexines. Two neighboring connexones build a connection of low resistance. That allows a direct flow of the action potential from one cell to the other. [23]

2.2.1.2 Neuroanatomy

On a very general level the neuronal structure of the brain can be divided in to two areas. When looking at a human brain cut into slices one can clearly see a grayish substance, called grey matter and white areas, the white matter. The grey matter mainly consists of cell bodies, dendrites, and axons, which are not covered by a myelin sheath. The white matter contains only of axons and most of them are covered by a myelin sheath. This area appears in white color because the myelin sheath consists of cell membrane layers that contain lipids. Because of the high concentration of lipids the whole area appears in the white color.

2.2.1.3 Cortical Organization of Neurons

In the central nervous system neurons are organized in functional structures. The concept of excitatory or inhibitory neurons is of essential importance for the understanding of the cortical organization. 80 % of all neurons in the cortex are excitatory pyramidal cells [137]. These cells are named after the pyramidal shape of their cell bodies. Pyramidal cells in the cortex are interconnected locally by axon collaterals and also with brain-areas outside the cortex. 90% of the pyramidal cell's axons connect to other cortical areas in both hemispheres. Association fibers form the ipsilateral connections and the contra-lateral connections are established via the corpus callosum by commissural fibers. This interconnection of excitatory neurons in the cortex forms a reverberation circuit [81], which makes it possible to prolong the activation of the cortex after a stimulus. The feed-forward and feed-back circuits recurrently activate each other leading to the prolonged activation.

The remaining pyramidal cells' axons connect with other parts of the brain outside the cortex. A special feature of pyramidal cells is their apical dendrite, which is a very long dendrite, 6 times longer than basal dendrites. These apical dendrites are oriented in a vertical organization, perpendicular to the cortical surface. This spacial orientation of the apical dendrites is a necessary prerequisite for the recording of the EEG. [23]

An other prominent type of neurons in the cortex are the mostly inhibitory stellate cells. They are inter-neurons that only connect locally and never leave the cortex. The stellate cells' dendrites are short and can process incoming signals fast and temporally precise

[81]. The major tasks of inhibitory neurons in the cortex are the prevention of over-excitation, the formation of complex receptive fields in the cortex, and the formation of comparison operators within the cortex.

Both types of neurons in the cortex, excitatory and inhibitory cells, receive excitatory signals originating in the thalamus. The thalamus contains multiple relay nuclei that act as a gate for signals from the sensory system [81].

2.2.1.4 Electrical Properties of Pyramidal Cells

Cortical Pyramidal cells have a resting potential of -50 mV to -80 mV. The action potential reaches an amplitude of 60 mV to 100 mV for a duration of 0.5 ms to 2 ms. It propagates from the axon hillock via the soma to the proximal apical dendrite. The activation of pyramidal cells can reach a frequency of 100 Hz.

Pyramidal cells form a dipole: The apical dendrite can be seen as the negative sink, the basal part of the cell as the positive source. The collective electrical behavior of cortical pyramidal cells can be measured by electrodes. This is the basis of EEG recording.

EPSPs have a duration of 10 ms to 30 ms, IPSPs have a longer duration of 70 ms to 150 ms. The spike of the action potential itself only lasts for 1 ms. EPSPs measured at apical dendrites can even have a duration in the range of seconds [23].

2.3 Measurement of Electrical Brain Activity

Electrical brain activity can be measured at various locations in and around the brain. A range of invasive methods exists to measure the activity of different layers inside the brain. Non-invasive methods are used to measure the activity from the outside of the brain.

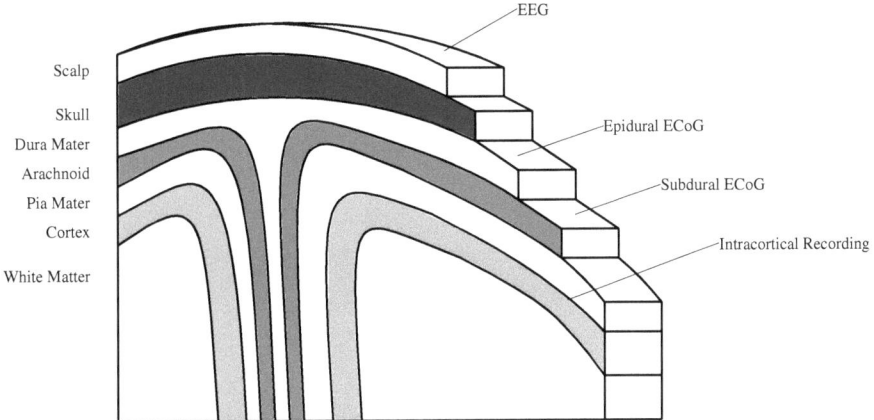

Figure 2.2: The layers of the brain on the left side and technologies to record electrical activity on the right side [88].

In figure 2.2 a schema of the layers of a human head is depicted. From outside towards the center these layers are

- the scalp, which is the skin covering
- the skull, which is the bone protecting the brain.
- The brain itself is covered by
- the dura mater,
- the arachnoid tissue, and
- the pia mater, which directly covers
- the cortex, which is the first layer actually containing neurons.

The dura mater is fixed to the skull, whereas the pia mater is fixed to the brain. The arachnoid layer compensates the movements of the brain relative to the skull. Due to the soft composition of the brain even small accelerations may lead to considerable movements of the brain.

On the right side of the figure different ways to measure electrical activity of the brain are shown. The layer where the activity is recorded is also indicated. The invasive technologies of intra-cortical electrode recordings and the electrocorticogram (ECoG) as well as the non-invasive electroencephalogram are explained in the following sections.

2.3.1 Invasive Recording of Electrical Activity

2.3.1.1 Intra-cortical Electrodes

The recording of electrical activity within cortical tissue dates back to the 1970ies. Fetz and Finoccio used single neuron recordings of monkeys to build a basic brain-computer-interface (BCI) system [53]. This research was the foundation for further research and experiments also in humans [76].

For the recording of the spiking activity of single neurons micro-electrodes with a tip-diameter of 20 μm are needed [105]. These electrodes are implanted some millimeters within the cortex. They are fixed relative to the brain and therefore move with the brain in the case of head movements.

A crucial issue of intra-cortical electrodes is the need to penetrate brain tissue. The electrode by itself causes local damage of tissue and may be the source of CNS infections. The chronic use of such invasive electrodes may lead to the formation of tissue at the site of the electrode-penetration. This tissue increases the resistance of the electrodes and can lead to a complete isolation of the electrode from the brain [105].

2.3.1.2 Electrocorticogram

In contrast to intra-cortical electrodes the electrocorticogram (ECoG) is recorded from electrodes that stay on the surface of the cortex and do not penetrate the cortical tissue. The ECoG is well suited to record summed up activity of a 'cortical column' of neurons as the orientation of most cortical neurons is perpendicular to the surface. As a consequence the cortical gyri are better recording positions than the sulci, where the neurons at these locations are parallel to the surface.

ECoG electrodes are frequently used in epilepsy-related surgery where the recordings are essential in the operating procedure. ECoG electrodes used in epilepsy monitoring have diameters in the range of millimeters. They cover a relatively large area of the cortex compared to the intracortical recordings.

As indicated in figure 2.2 two types of ECoG recordings exist:

- Subdural ECoG is recorded under the dura mater layer. The recording happens inside the CNS and may therefore be a source of infection. The movement of the brain described earlier may lead to additional irritations when using subdural ECoG [105].
- Epidural ECoG electrodes stay on the outside of the dura and circumvent these problems. The position of the electrodes has a better protection regarding the immune system of the brain, but also increases the distance to the neurons. In general the signal quality of subdural and epidural ECoG recordings do not differ significantly [105].

2.3.2 Electroencephalography

Electroencephalography (EEG) is a non-invasive way to measure the electrical activity of the brain's cortex and hippocampus by placing electrodes on the scalp.

The first scientific publication about electrical brain activity dates back to 1875 [36] and was published by Richard Caton. He was the first to experiment with a galvanometer measuring electric currents in animal brains. Half a decade later the invention of suitable electronic amplifiers made Caton's discovery more useful.

Electrical activity from the scalp of a human was first recorded by Hans Berger in 1924 at the University of Jena in Germany. He also discovered the non-randomness of theses potentials, which showed irregularities as well as periodicities [21]. Berger also invented the term "electroencephalogram" [1]. One of his early EEG recordings is shown in figure 2.3

Berger's publication [21] was verified years later in 1934 by Adrian and Mathews [4]. This led to a further acceptance of the concept of 'brain waves'. The activity in the 10 Hz to 12 Hz frequency range was initially called 'Berger rhythm'. Adrian and Mathews coined the term 'alpha rhythm'. They also discovered the attenuation of alpha activity by

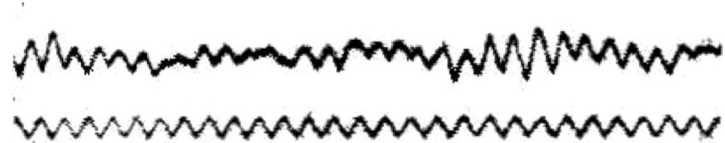

Figure 2.3: This figure shows an early EEG recorded by Hans Berger in 1924. The upper signal is the EEG, the lower a 10 Hz sinus wave [21].

focused attention and alertness.

2.3.2.1 EEG Recording

The EEG is recorded by placing electrodes on the scalp. The electrical neural activity of the brain can be measured by recording the potential difference between two electrodes [1]. Two ways of measuring the potential differences are commonly used:

- Monopolar EEG recordings measure the difference between an electrode placed on the scalp and a reference electrode. The reference electrodes are usually placed at a relatively neutral point that is not influenced by muscle and brain activity, for instance the ear or the mastoid, which is the area begin the ear. Monopolar recordings are also called referential recordings.
- Bipolar EEG recordings use two electrodes placed on the scalp. A third electrode is used as ground electrode. The difference between the two scalp electrodes is measured. This leads to a 'common-mode rejection', which ensures an intrinsic artifact cancellation. This way of measuring can produce biased signals that do not represent the actual brain activity but the non-physiological result of an arithmetic subtraction.

2.3.2.1.1 Electrode Placement The electrode placement is crucial to obtain comparable and reproducible results. For this purpose the Federation in Electroencephalography and Clinical Neurophysiology introduced the '10-20 electrode placement system' in 1958 [151], which is schematically shown in figure 2.4. The electrodes are placed relatively to two anatomical landmarks, the nasion and the inion. The nasion is the lower-lying point between the eyes, the inion is the outstanding bone at the backside of the skull. The

2.3 Measurement of Electrical Brain Activity

electrodes are placed in a grid of one 10% step, four 20% steps, and another 10% step from the left to the right and from the nasion to inion. The electrodes are placed on grid's confluences. Each of them has a unique name according to a scheme consisting of a letter and an index number.

The letters represent the name of the anatomical areas:

- A, the ear lobes.
- M, mastoid, the bone behind the ears.
- C, the central area of the skull.
- Pg, the nasopharyngeal area.
- P, the parietal areas.
- F, the frontal area.
- Fp, the frontal polar area.
- T, the temporal areas.
- O, the occipital area.

The electrodes on the left hemisphere have odd number indices, the electrodes on the right have even numbers, which increase starting at the central line between nasion and inion. The electrodes on the central line exceptionally have the index z.

2.3.2.1.2 Electrodes Silver chloride (Ag-AgCl) disks with a diameter of 1 mm to 3 mm are most commonly used as electrodes to acquire EEG signals from the scalp. To improve the signal quality a low impedance at the skin-electrode interface is desirable (<10 $k\Omega$ [26]). For this purpose the skin can be abraded by using special pastes. Usually the skin is disinfected with for instance alcohol to avoid skin irritations. Conductive paste or contact cement can help to improve the conditions of this interface before placing the electrode itself.

Collodion is another substance, which can be used to keep electrodes in place. Collodion has very strong adhesive properties and even needs a dissolvent fluid to be removed. In the clinical practice collodion is therefore used for subjects that suffer from conditions which make normal conductive paste not usable, for instance grand mal epileptic seizures or extreme transpiration.

22 Electrical Brain Activity

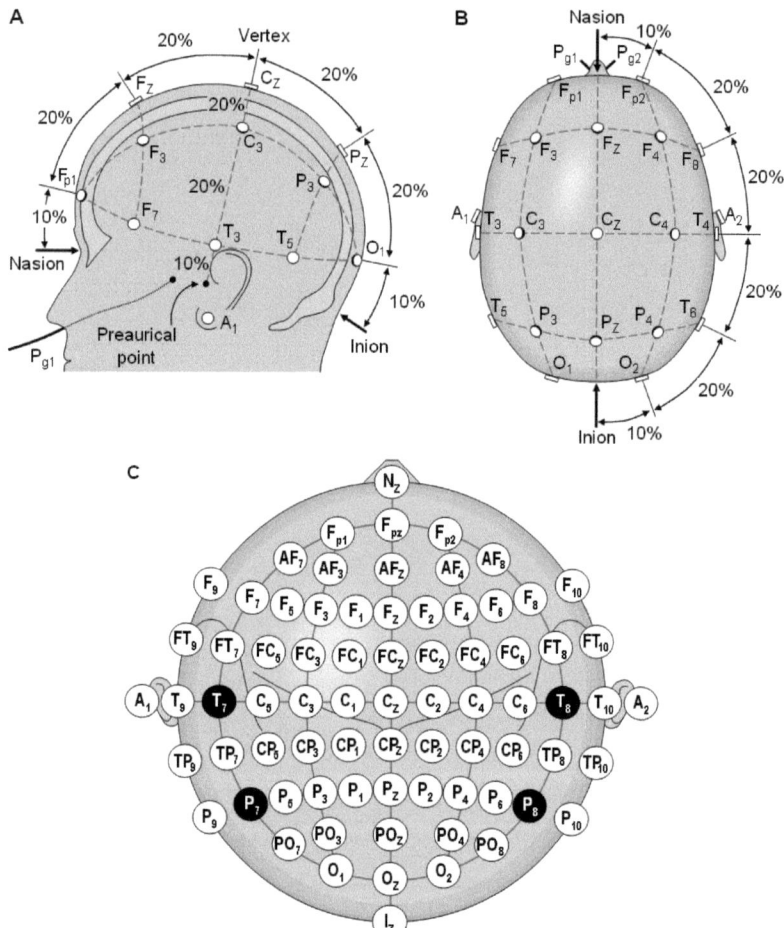

Figure 2.4: Schamtic visualization of the international 10-20 electrode placement system. Figure A shows a saggital view of a human head. The 10 % and 20 % steps from the nasion to the inion are shown. The superior head view in figure B shows the central line between nasion and inion as well as both hemispheres with the add and even location numbering. In figure C a planar schema of the the whole scalp is visualized showing the complete 10-20 electrode scheme. The figures are taken from [100].

Another type of electrodes, which are slightly more invasive, are needle electrodes. They are are inserted below the skin and are used for long-term recordings [151].

2.3 Measurement of Electrical Brain Activity

An example of a recently published EEG recording device is the neuro-headset 'Epoc' from the Australian company Emotiv Systems. The device is shown in figure 2.5. The wireless device is based on a proprietary wireless protocol that uses the 2.4 GHz frequency band. It can record 14 EEG channels from frontal, temporal, occipital, and parietal positions according to the 10-20 electrode placement system. The battery lasts for 12 hours and the system together with the proprietary software libraries works in real-time. An embedded gyroscope helps to detect and remove movement artifacts. The electrodes are based on 'felt pads' that have to be moistened with a saline solution. Like this the electrodes are capable of recording EEG activity even if they are placed on the subject's hair. The main advantage of the wireless solution is the removal of wires and the corresponding artifacts, as explained in section 2.4.1. The subject can move freely within the range of the wireless reception. This allows a wide range of real-world applications. The device is not certified for clinical use.

Figure 2.5: The Epoc wireless neuro-headset from Emotive Systems. The image is taken from the company's website emotiv.com.

2.3.2.1.3 Amplification, Sampling, and Digitalization With carefully applied electrodes amplitudes of 1 μV to 10 μV can be measured, which is too less for a direct further processing. An amplification in the order of 10^6 is necessary.

Analogue technology was used in the early days of signal recording. Non-digital conservative recording techniques are pen or chart recorders that draw multiple EEG channels on a continuous sheet of paper. Usually the speed of the paper can be adapted in such system, which leads to different temporal resolutions. An other analogue way to record EEG data is the use of a frequency modulated tape recorder. An oscilloscope or a video display can be used to display the EEG using the tape recorder.

Nowadays the usual way of recording biosignals is digital. At a certain rate, the sample or sampling rate, the analogous value of the system is measured and converted to a digital representation by using an analogue/digital (A/D) converter.

In order to choose a suitable sampling rate for a recording, the Nyquist–Shannon sampling theorem has to be taken into account:

"If a function f(t) contains no frequencies higher than W cps [cycles per second, Hertz], it is completely determined by giving its ordinates at a series of points spaced 1/2 W seconds apart." [143]

As a consequence the sampling frequency has to be chosen higher than two times the highest frequency needed for the signal analysis.

The result of digitalization is a time series of discrete scalar values, which can be expressed as the function $x(n)$ with n representing the index of the sampled value. The digital representation of a value has a limited value range that depends on the number of available bits. The A/D converter has a certain range of output values. For an output range of $\pm$ 5V a 12 bit digital representation would not be enough to represent all possible values. 12 bit can only represent $\pm$ 2.4 mV. It is therefore crucial to correctly parametrize the signal amplification, the A/D conversion, and digitalization [26] in order to record valid signals.

2.4 Analysis of EEG Signals

In this section an overview of the challenges and possibilities of the analysis of the EEG is given. The possibilities of analysis also depend on the way of EEG processing and recording.

2.4.1 EEG Artifacts

Any effect recorded in a signal that is of another origin than the intended recording source is considered to be an artifact. In the case of EEG: anything but electrical brain activity is considered to be an artifact.

In many applications of the EEG artifacts are considered as unwanted influences, but they can also be seen as additional phenomena that may help to interpret the measured activity [108]. In any case it is crucial to be able to detect artifacts correctly in order to clearly distinguish between the artifacts and the actual brain activity.

Artifacts can be categorized into two groups [141]. One group of artifacts are of physiological nature and produced by the body, for instance eye movements, facial muscle movements, or the typical pattern of the heart beat. The second type of artifacts are of environmental origin, such as the line noise of the alternating current. Depending on the region of the world it is either 50 Hz or 60 Hz.

2.4.1.1 Physiological EEG Artifacts

2.4.1.1.1 Muscle Activity Muscle activity is the most common artifact in the EEG. The major reason for that the electrical signal produced by muscle activity lies in the range of millivolts, whereas the measurable brain activity outside the skull lies in the range of microvolts. Muscle Artifacts may be present in the EEG when the subject is moving, is 'tense', or uses any facial muscles while speaking, eating, laughing, etc. When dealing with patients several disorders may also be the reason for muscle artifacts, for instance Parkinson's disease or any other kind of tremor [141].

Muscle artifacts in the EEG have a frequency range of 20 Hz to 100 Hz. This frequency range overlaps with the classical EEG frequency bands beta and gamma (see section

2.4.2.2). Theoretically muscle activity could be removed from the EEG by applying a lowpass filter removing all high frequencies. Such a filter potentially also removes actual brain activity leading to distortions in further EEG processing, for instance a statistical analysis of the signal. It is therefore not recommended to use the parts of the EEG signal that are affected by muscle artifacts for further EEG processing.

2.4.1.1.2 Glossokinetic Activity This kind of activity of artifact in the EEG has its origin in the movement of the tongue. The tongue has a potential difference between the tip and the base, which represents a dipole. Glossokinetic artifacts are present in subjects that are in a wake state and the artifacts vanish during drowsiness and sleep. The presence of glossokinetic activity in the EEG can be an indicator that the subject is swallowing, chewing, or speaking [141].

Nam et al. [108] propose the use of glossokinetic artifacts in the EEG to build a tongue-machine interface. They experimentally show that they can correctly interpret the tongue position in the mouth by implementing a tongue-based cursor control interface. Their signal analysis relies on principal component analysis.

2.4.1.1.3 Eye Movements Eye movements appear in the EEG as artifacts. The origin of this electrical activity is the potential difference between the eye's retina and the cornea, which forms a dipole and leads to a similar effect as the glossokinetic activity. In comparison to the retina, the cornea is positively charged and the potential difference is about 6 mV. The negativity of the retina is caused by the high density of sensory cells that react to light. As a consequence the potential difference depends on the light intensity. The movement of these dipoles can also be measured directly by placing electrodes next to the eyes. The resulting biosignal is called the electrooculogram (EOG) . A schematic visualization of the EOG can be found in figure 2.6. The recording of the EOG can help to detect and remove EOG artifacts in the EEG [141].

Eye movement artifacts appear especially in the EEG channels near the eyes that are the frontal and fronto-polar channels. Eye blinks also appear in the EEG as artifacts. A blink causes a vertical eye movement clearly visible in the EEG, especially in the fronto-polar channels. The vertical movement of the eyes during lid closure is called 'Bell phenomenon' [141].

2.4 Analysis of EEG Signals 27

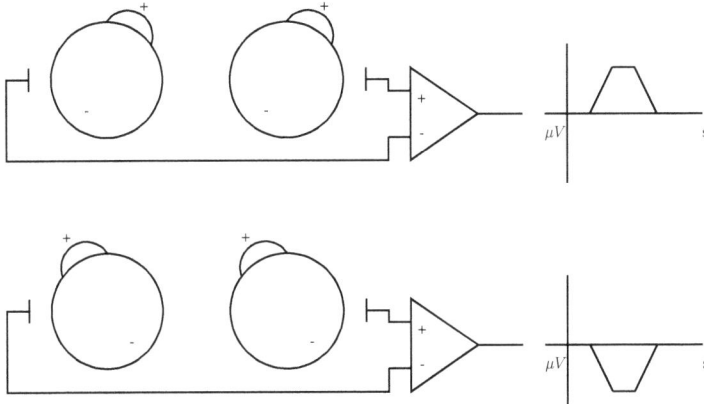

Figure 2.6: Schematic figure of the recording setup of the EOG. In the left part of the figure two eyes are depicted with two electrodes at the left and right side, the outer canthi. On the right side of the figure the resulting potential differences are visualized. While the eye is in a resting state no voltage is recorded. With the rotation of the two eyes this state changes. In the upper part the two eyes look to the right, resulting in a positive voltage in the lower part the eyes look to the left resulting in a negative EOG signal.

2.4.1.1.4 Heart Activity In some subjects the electrocardiogram (ECG), the heart's muscular activity, can be detected as an artifact in the EEG. Some EEG electrode montages, such as the referential montage using the ear positions A1 and A2, are more prone to record an ECG artifact than others [141].

The pulse is a direct consequence of the hearts pumping activity. Pulse artifacts can occur, when EEG electrodes are placed directly over vessels. Pulse artifacts can be distinguished from other EEG phenomena, as they only appear in single channels with misplaced electrodes.

The EEG of subjects with pace makers can contain additional artifacts. The pace maker represents an additional electrical source in the subject's body that may influence the EEG recordings.

2.4.1.1.5 Skin Effects Stable skin conditions are optimal for EEG recording. Unfortunately these conditions may change, especially during long-term recordings. Sweat changes the impedance of the skin and may even interact electrically with the electrodes. The resulting artifacts in the EEG are very low frequent baseline changes at frequencies between 0.25 Hz and 0.5 Hz [141].

2.4.1.2 Environmental EEG Artifacts

Artifacts that have their source outside the subject's body are considered as environmental artifacts. Such effects are mainly of technical nature and introduced by the surrounding, such as other medical equipment or the EEG recording system itself.

2.4.1.2.1 Electrodes The electrodes and their fixation on the skin may be a source of artifacts. Usually the electrodes are fixed by using sticky gels, sticky patches, plastic caps, or other mechanical fixation systems. Instable or sub-optimally placed electrodes lead to a high impedance of the skin-electrode interface. The movement of such electrodes leads to a quick recharge of a local potential resulting in 'electrode pop' artifacts. They become visible as sharp spikes followed by a decay towards the channel's baseline [141].

An additional source of artifacts are the movements of the electrode's cables. Such movements can additionally alter the recorded signal.

2.4.1.2.2 Alternating Current A common problem in biosignal recording is the electromagnetic field generated by alternating current of the power lines surrounding the subject and the recording system. Depending on the world's region the power grid's current alternates at a frequency of 50 Hz or 60 Hz. The frequency is confined to exactly 50 Hz or 60 Hz and the artifact can safely be removed by filtering the affected frequency band.

2.4.1.2.3 Intravenous Artifacts A very special artifact is the 'drip' artifact introduced by intravenous treatments. This is a condition that usually occurs in EEG recordings in the intensive care unit. The dripping of some medicine may cause sharp periodic spikes in the EEG [141].

2.4.2 Analysis of Frequencies

2.4.2.1 Time Domain and Frequency Domain

The most common way of EEG signal analysis is the analysis in the frequency domain. The idea of the analysis of the frequency contents of a time series goes back to 1807. Joseph Fourier presented the idea of expressing any 'arbitrary periodic signal' [51] as a sum of sinus and cosine functions. If frequencies and amplitudes of the cosine and sine function are chosen correctly, the original signal can be reconstructed by the sum of those functions. This idea can be expressed as the term

$$x(t) = a_0 + \sum_{m=1}^{\infty} (a_m cos(m\omega_0 t) + b_m sin(m\omega_0 t)).$$

a_m and b_m represent the amplitude of each frequency $\omega_m = m\omega_0$. ω_0 is the function's fundamental frequency in radians / s [51].

Based on this idea a signal can either be expressed in the time domain or in the frequency domain. The original idea of Fourier series is intended for periodic signals. Biosignals such as the EEG are signals that do not fulfill this property. To be able to apply Fourier's idea anyway the concept has to be extended. The Fourier transform can be applied to the non-periodic signal to decompose it to its frequency components

$$X(\omega) = \int_{-\infty}^{\infty} x(t)e^{-j\omega t} dt.$$

$X(\omega)$ is a complex function of the frequency ω. The same principle works also in the other way, the original signal can be restored by its frequency components

$$x(t) = \frac{1}{2\pi} \int_{-\infty}^{\infty} X(\omega)e^{-j\omega t} d\omega.$$

As biosignals are usually sampled and digitalized, they are only available as a series of discrete scalar values. The discrete Fourier transform is used to handle these value series

$$X(m) = \sum_{k=0}^{N-1} x(k)e^{-j\pi mkN^{-1}}$$

$m = 0, 1, ..., N/2$ represents the 'digital' frequency index and N the even number of samples in the transformed window of the signal. Depending on the sample rate this 'digital' frequency can be transformed to the real frequency in Hertz. $x(k)$ is the digitalized biosignal.

The inverse discrete Fourier transform is defined as

$$x(k) = \frac{1}{N} \sum_{k=0}^{N-1} X(m) e^{j\pi m k N^{-1}} \text{ with } k = 0, 1, ... N - 1.$$

The exact explanation of these transforms can be found in any digital signal processing text book. The two representations of a signal - the time domain and the frequency domain - are interchangeable in the continuous as well as in the discrete version.

2.4.2.2 EEG Frequency Bands

A range of frequencies can be bundled together to form a frequency band. A specialty of the EEG is the definition and usage of certain frequency bands that have unique names. These bands are not chosen arbitrarily but stand for different states of the brain.

- The delta (δ) band contains frequencies up to 4 Hz. It is the band with the slowest frequencies in the EEG and it is most prevalent in adults during slow wave sleep. An example for this kind of delta activity can be found in figure 2.7. Delta activity is also typical in babies' EEG.
- The theta (θ) band is defined in the range of 4 Hz to 8 Hz. The presence of theta activity is typical for drowsiness in adults. Theta activity is known to be present in children during wakefulness.
- The historically first described frequency band was the alpha (α) band. The most common range used is from 8 Hz to 13 Hz. Most adults in a relaxed state with closed eyes show alpha activity in their EEG. Usually alpha activity attenuates when opening the eyes and with attention and increased alertness.
- Beta (β) is the name of the frequency band between 13 Hz and 30 Hz. Beta activity in adults is usually interpreted as a state of alertness, thinking, and concentration.
- The frequencies above 30 Hz are usually called gamma (γ) band. Because of the damping of the electrical signal by the skull, the power of the gamma frequency components is very low and therefore very hard to distinguish from a signal artifacts. Nevertheless some authors associate gamma activity with sensory processing and memory matching. A decrease in gamma activity is interpreted as a cognitive decline.
- The mu (μ) rhythm is a sub-band defined in the range between 8 Hz and 13 Hz. It is only used for EEG signals from the sensorimotor cortex and represents the resting

2.4 Analysis of EEG Signals 31

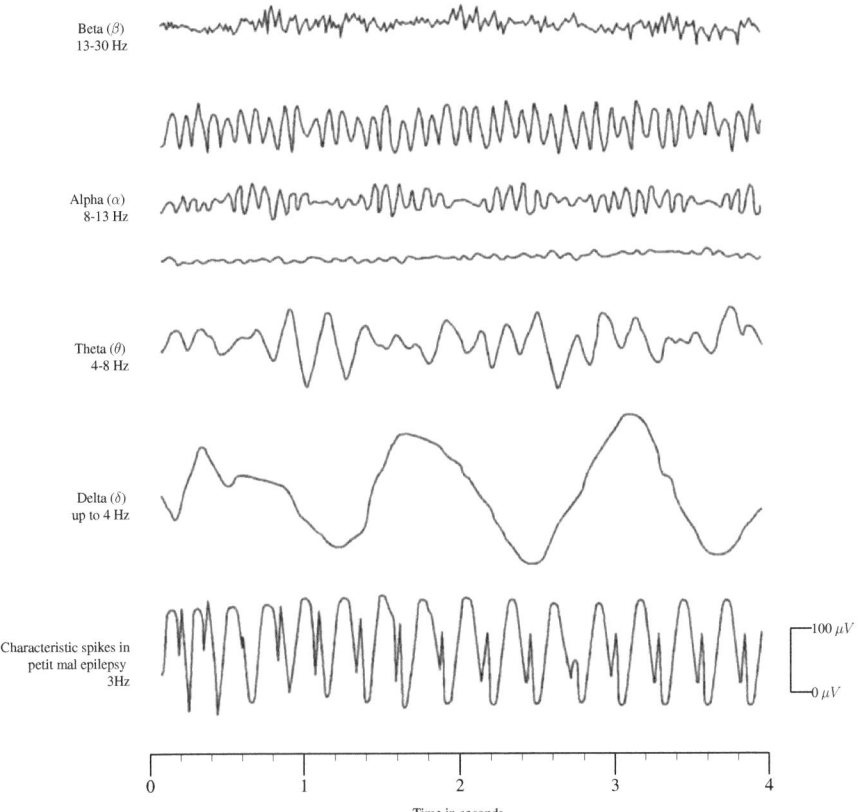

Figure 2.7: This figure shows some example of typical EEG frequency components. The uppermost figure shows a beta rhythm, the next three signals are alpha rhythms, the fifth signals is a typical theta rhythm, and the sixth shows high amplitude delta waves. The last signals shows characteristic epileptic spikes. This figure is taken from [100].

state of motor neurons.

- A special sub-band is the sigma (σ) band, which lies between 12 Hz and 14 Hz. It is synonymously used for sleep spindles, which are a transient phenomenon in the Rechtschaffen and Kales sleep stage 2.

2.4.2.3 Power Spectral Density

The spectral density, or power spectral density (PSD), is a widely used function, which represents the frequency content of a signal. In contrast to the Fourier transform the PSD is a positive real function and has the unit 'power per Hertz'. For biosignals that are measured in Volts the PSD is given in $V^2 Hz^{-1}$. It is often called spectrum or frequency power of a signal [127].

For a sampled and digitalized biosignal $f_n = f(ndt)$ with $1 \leq n \leq N$ measured for the time $T = ndt$ the PSD is defined as

$$PSD(m) = \frac{dt^2}{T} \left| \sum_{n=1}^{N} f_n e^{-imn} \right|^2 \text{ [127]}.$$

m stands for the digital frequency that can be converted to the real frequency in Hertz by using the sampling rate.

2.4.3 Filtering

Filtering is an essential technique in signal processing. In this thesis we want to give a short overview of the terminology used. The theoretical and technical details of filters can be found in any signal processing textbook [127].

Depending on the result of a filter, a number of filter types exists. The most frequently used types are [127]:

- A lowpass filter cuts off frequencies above a defined cutoff frequency. Only low frequencies pass.
- The highpass filter is the opposite of the lowpass filter. Frequencies higher than the cutoff frequency pass, the others are attenuated.
- A bandpass filter is the combination of lowpass and highpass filter. All frequencies below and above a defined frequency band are attenuated.
- A bandstop filter eliminates a certain frequency band. A notch filter is an extreme case of a bandstop filter that attenuates only a very narrow frequency band. It is typically used to eliminate the mains hum from biosignals which is exactly either 50 Hz or 60 Hz.

2.4.4 Analysis in the Time Domain

Besides the analysis of the EEG in the frequency domain there are also some ways to analyze the signal in the time domain.

There are simple statistical measures that can be applied to the signal, in most cases to time-windows of the signal [27].

2.4.4.1 Arithmetic Mean

The mean of the raw EEG signal is a very small value, as the raw signal consists of negative and positive values. A change in the mean of a window of a raw EEG signal is most likely of technical nature, for instance drifts in the amplifier [27].

In contrast, the mean of the absolute values of the raw signal can have an other meaning. For example the mean of the absolute values of the band-filtered EEG signal can be used as a simple means to measure the contribution of the frequency band to the EEG.

2.4.4.2 Median and Quantiles

The median is often preferred over the mean if the data to be analyzed has a large number of extreme values or is not normally distributed. The median is more robust concerning such data and the value gets close to the mean when it is applied to normally distributed data [27].

The median value is defined as the 50 % quantile. Quantiles are also applied to EEG data, for instance for defining statistically dynamic thresholds. In many publications a defined data range is used as the reference data for a recording session or a subject. This reference data then serves to define statistical thresholds, for instance to cut off outliers or to define events.

An example application of this idea is the extraction of events in the alpha band. The event-like character in the alpha band can be seen in the third signal of figure 2.7. The absolute values of the band filtered data are used as the basis of the calculation. If a section of the data has higher amplitudes than for instance the 80 % quantile of the reference data the section is defined as a alpha-event. A statistically relative definition of a threshold has the advantage that the algorithm automatically adapts to inter-subject and inter-session differences in the amplitude of the recorded data.

2.4.4.3 Standard Deviation

In some cases the standard deviation of an EEG signal is used as an EEG-based variable, especially the standard deviation of a frequency band filtered EEG signal. To calculate the standard deviation of a sample the following formula can be used

$$S_N = \sqrt{\frac{1}{N} \sum_{i=1}^{N} (x_i - mean(X))^2}.$$

X represents the vector of values x_i with $i = 1..N$.

A more suitable version of the calculation of the standard deviation is the 'sample standard deviation'

$$S = \sqrt{\frac{1}{N-1} \sum_{i=1}^{N} (x_i - mean(X))^2}.$$

The so called 'Bessel's correction' is an unbiased estimator for the variance of the underlying population, if the sample values are independent (with replacement). In this case the standard deviation of samples with $N = 1$ stays undefined, which corresponds to the natural understanding of this measure [27].

2.4.4.4 Skewness

A measure for the deviation from the normal distribution is called the skewness. A deviation from a symmetric histogram of an EEG-signal may indicate the presence of monophasic events, such as spikes. A way to calculate the skewness is Pearson's second coefficient of skewness

$$Skewness = \frac{3(mean(X) - median(X))}{standard deviation(X)}$$

where X stands for the vector of EEG values in the chosen window [27].

2.4.5.5 Kurtosis

A measure of 'peakedness' [27] of the EEG signal is called kurtosis. Applied to the EEG a high value of kurtosis points to the presence of spikes and events with high amplitudes. The kurtosis can be calculated the following way:

$$K = \frac{\sum_{i=1}^{N} \frac{(x_i - mean(X))^4}{N}}{\sum_{i=1}^{N} \left(\frac{(x_i - mean(X))^2}{N}\right)^2} - 3.$$

2.4.5 Complexity Measures

The measurement of the 'complexity' of a signal is a topic that appears in several scientific fields. In biomedical engineering the complexity of an ECG is used to distinguish the heart's signal from health and ill hearts, complexity measures are used for the analysis of DNA sequences and also manufacturing processes are analyzed using complexity measures citeBandt2002. Depending on the scientific field the term complexity can can have several meanings. The most suitable definition in this context is complexity as a 'measure of randomness'.

In information theory entropy is used as a measure of information content. The unpredictability of a sequence of symbols is expressed by the entropy rate 'h'. The unit is usually given in bits per symbol.

For a random variable X with n outcomes $x_1 \ldots x_n$ the entropy is defined as $H(X)$.

$$H(X) = \sum_{i=1}^{n} p(x_i) log_b \frac{1}{p(x_i)} = -\sum_{i=1}^{n} p(x_i) log_b (p(x_i)).$$

$p(x_i)$ is the probability mass function. The base of the logarithm b defines the name of the unit: for $b = 2$ the unit is bit, for $b = e$ its nat, and for $b = 10$ its dit [2].

For a coin flip the entropy is 1 bit, assuming a probability of 0.5 that the coin lands on the one or the other side.

2.4.5.1 Permutation Entropy Index

The Permutation Entropy Index (PEI) was introduced by Bandt and Pompe [20] in 2002 as a 'natural complexity measure for time series'. It has a direct applicability to real-world time series even in presence of dynamic or observational noise.

The PEI is defined for a time series $\{x_t\}$ with $t = 1...T$. The PEI is based on the comparison of neighboring values. The differences between the values x_t are calculated and it is evaluated whether the differences are positive or negative. For each n differences the sequence of positive or negative differences is analyzed, for instance for $n = 3$ a sequence could be 'positive, negative, negative'. All possible sequences, or patterns, and their application to a biosignal are illustrated in figure 2.8.

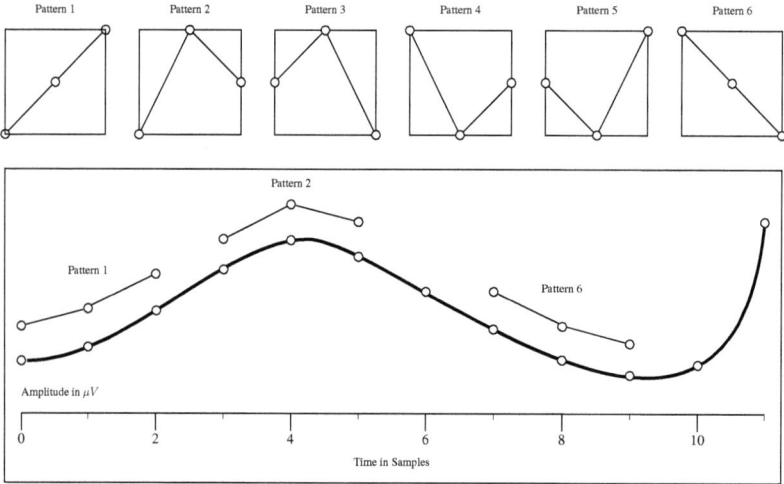

Figure 2.8: This figure illustrates the basic algorithm of the Permutation Entropy. The six possible patterns of a permutation of n=3 are shown in the upper part of the figure. In the lower part these patterns are matched to an exemplary biosignal [20].

Regarding the whole time series the PEI analyzes $n!$ permutations of order n. For each permutation π a relative frequency is calculated:

2.4 Analysis of EEG Signals

$$p(\pi) = \frac{\#\{t|0 \leq t \leq T - n, (x_{t+1}, ..., x_{t+n}) \text{ has type } \pi\}}{T - n + 1}.$$

With these prerequisites the permutation entropy is defined as

$$H(n) = -\sum p(\pi) log(p(\pi)).$$

The result lies in the value range of $0 \leq H(n) \leq log(n!)$.

2.5 Applications of the EEG

EEG recording and interpretation is a standard procedure in the clinical routine and is used for a wide range of applications. In this section we present the major clinical applications of EEG and other important applications in related fields.

2.5.1 Epilepsy

EEG recordings play an important role in the diagnosis and treatment of epilepsy. To optimally diagnose a seizure disorder it is necessary to record an EEG during a seizure event. In the clinical practice the EEG of epileptic patients is recorded only for 20 minutes. Because of this short timespan it is very unlikely to actually capture a seizure [150].

As a consequence clinicians rely on changes in the EEG between seizure, the so called interictal EEG. It is known that a high number of patients with epileptic seizures have a significantly altered interictal EEG with phenomena such as transient spikes or sharp waves [150]. This 'epileptiform activity' consists of transient phenomena in the EEG that are clearly distinct from the normal EEG. Abnormal epileptiform activity does not necessarily happen in the course of an actual seizure. It can be observed in 40% to 60% of subjects suffering from seizures [47] and in 1% of subjects that are considered to be healthy [171].

Besides the use of the EEG for a general diagnosis, the EEG can also help in clarifying the types of seizures, for instance complex partial seizures and absence seizures. In most subjects with absence seizures epileptiform waves can be induced by hyperventilation. Sharp waves and spikes are seen more frequently in patients with complex partial seizures. The ability to distinguish types of seizures also helps to choose the right medication, which are mostly anticonvulsant drugs. The influence of medication on the interictal EEG is disputed in literature. Medication may stop the actual seizures but does not normalize the interictal EEG [150].

2.5.2 LORETA

Low Resolution Brain Electromagnetic Tomography (LORETA) [120, 121] is an EEG-based functional brain-imaging technology. It aims to use the advantages of EEG over other technologies in the field of imaging. Other functional imaging methods rely on the brain's metabolism, such as positron emission tomography (PET) or functional magnetic resonance imaging (fMRI). The spacial resolution of these methods is very good, but the delay of measuring events and effects may be up to 5 seconds, as it is the case for fMRI, which is based on the BOLD effect.

In contrast to those imaging methods EEG can be recorded and processed with nearly no latency, but has a limited spacial resolution. LORETA is an EEG signal processing algorithm that aims at using EEG signals for functional brain imaging.

It relies on the idea that the activity recorded using the EEG is generated by electrical sources which are distributed in the brain. This idea can be expressed as the 'EEG forward problem'. It assumes that the sources of electrical activity in the brain are known and the signals generated at the surface of the brain can be calculated. In general the solution to this problem is well defined. LORETA is based on the assumption that the sources of activity are voxels (cubic pixels) arranged on a regular cubic matrix, which is visualized in figure 2.9.

The EEG forward problem can be formalized as

$$\Phi = KJ.$$

Where Φ is a vector a length n that represents the EEG measurements. $J = (j_1^T, j_2^T, \ldots j_m^T)^T$ is the vector of current densities j at m locations in the brain volume. K is a transfer matrix that represents the lead field [121].

The aim of LORETA is to solve the 'EEG inverse problem', which is the opposite of the EEG forward problem. On the basis of EEG signals the generators of the activity should be calculated. There is no general solution to this problem. Even an infinite number of EEG signals is not sufficient to find a unique distribution of generators that explains the projection.

LORETA's solution to the EEG inverse problem relies on the idea that the electrical generators are not randomly distributed in the brain, but follow the neuro-anatomical and

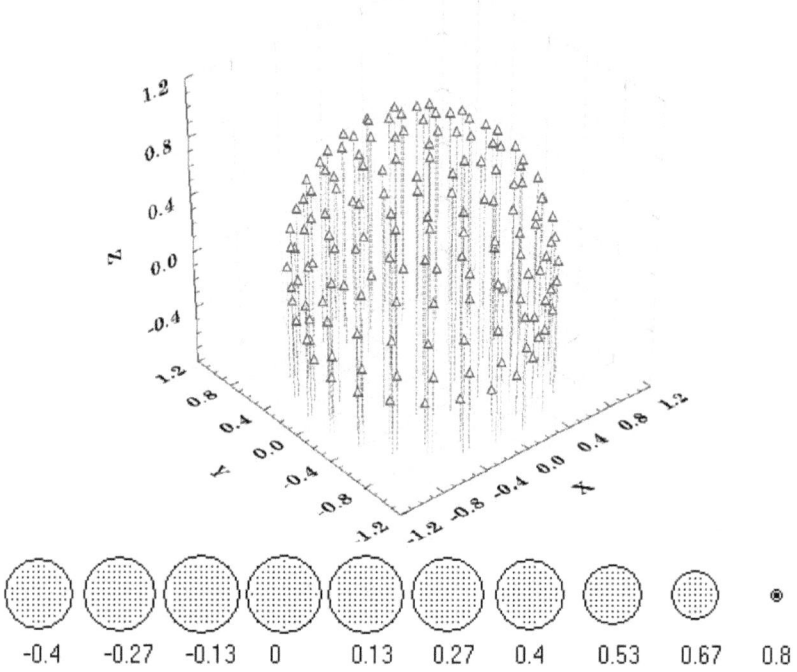

Figure 2.9: The first figure shows a cubic representation of the EEG scalp electrodes. The second figure shows the LORETA solution spac, consisting of regularly arranged voxels. Figures taken from [117].

electro-physiological constraints of the brain. These constraints are sufficient to find a unique solution to the problem. LORETA's approach relies mainly on the fact that the EEG signals measured on the scalp are the result of the synchronous activity of a large number of neurons with a perpendicular orientation towards the surface. To solve the problem LORETA assumes that there is a strong synchronization of neighboring neurons. This constraint of finding the smoothest current density can be formalized as

$\min_{J} \|BWJ\|^2$ under the constraint that the forward definition $\Phi = KJ$ is still true. $Z = WJ = (z_1^T, z_2^T, \ldots z_m^T)^T$, where z is the weighted current density and $BZ = (l_1^T, l_2^T, \ldots l_m^T)^T$ is a discrete laplacian. This laplacian operator is LORETA's way to ex-

2.5 Applications of the EEG

press the smoothness constraint. It is defined as

$$l_i = \frac{1}{d^2}(6z_i - \sum_p z_p)\forall p,$$

under the constraint that the distance of the coordinates r_i and r_p is equal the defined inter-point distance $d = \|r_i - r_p\|$ [121]. The Laplace operator represents the divergence of the gradient and can be understood as a local measure of 'outgoingness'. According to the 'Theory of application of constrained inverse of matrices' by Rao and Mitra [128] the unique solution for T can be calculated, which is needed of the solution estimate of the EEG inverse problem

$$J^* = T\Phi.$$

To further improve the results of LORETA's solutions to the EEG inverse problem the solution space is limited to the anatomically plausible structures, the cortical gray matter and the hippo-campus. LORETA uses a spherical head model and coordinates according to the Tailrach human brain atlas [149]. The Talairach coordinate system is relative to two reference points, the anterior and the posterior commissure. This way the coordinate system is independent of subject's individual difference in brain size.

LORETA was validated by experimental data with known solutions and by using empirical data. A successful example of the application of LORETA is the publication of Anderer et al. [16]. The authors apply LORETA to find the origin of sleep spindles, which are a transient phenomenon during sleep. They could identify two sleep spindle generators that are frequency specific. One generates slow sleep spindles with less than 13 Hz the second generator is responsible for faster sleep spindles with more than 13 Hz. Their findings are consistent with earlier publications using different approaches.

After being criticized and discussed by the scientific community LORETA was further improve, leading to standardized LORETA (sLORETA) in 2002 [118]. It removes the localization bias in the presence of measurement or biological noise. Exact LORETA (eLORETA) was published in 2007 [119] and is able to reduce the localization bias even further.

2.5.3 Brain Computer Interfaces

The basic idea of Brain Computer Interfaces (BCI) is the interpretation of brain-activity as control signals. BCI introduces an additional or alternative way of communication to the human body. It circumvents the natural way of peripheral nerves and the motor pathways [61]. By definition, a real BCI has four components:

- The signal source must be the brain in a direct way, either involving invasive or non-invasive technologies, as explained in section 2.3.
- The subject has to be provided with a feedback. This is seen as an essential feature of a BCI system [61].
- A BCI system has to act in real-time without introducing any delays.
- The signals interpreted by the BCI as control commands have to be produced intentionally by the subject.

A common way to acquire brain signals for a BCI system is the EEG. The same advantages and disadvantages mentioned in section 2.3 apply. The successful acquisition of the brain signal is one necessary prerequisite for a functional BCI system together with the successful detection and/or removal of artifacts.

The next step of BCI relies on the detection of specific patterns in the signal. The subject itself has to intentionally generate these patterns by following so called 'mental strategies'. This strategy defines the subject's necessary actions to successfully generate distinguishable and specific patterns in the brain's signal. The choice of the mental strategy also determines the amount of necessary training. Two mental strategies are the most commonly applied: focused attention and motor imagery [61]. Cecotti et al. [37] explain the application of these two strategies to a BCI based spelling interface.

2.5.3.1 Focused Attention

Selective or focused attention as a mental strategy for BCI relies on the presence of external stimuli that have to be provided by the BCI system. Such stimuli can be visual, auditory, or of any other somatosensory form. Most commonly flashing lights are used as stimuli, but there are also systems employing tones or tactile stimuli .

2.5 Applications of the EEG

Evoked Potentials Visually evoked potentials (VEP) are a clearly visible pattern in the EEG, which happens at a certain delay after a stimulus, for instance the P300 VEP is a positive wave about 300 milliseconds after a visual stimulus. The BCI algorithm has to correctly associate the presented stimuli to the brain's reactions. This association has to happen with a very low latency [61].

A possible scenario are symbols on a screen that represent commands. The symbols blink at distinct times and the subject concentrates on one of the symbols. Every time the symbol blinks the algorithm can detect the corresponding VEP in the subject's brain signal [23].

Steady-State Visual Evoked Potentials SSVEPs rely on a similar principle. Instead of distinct blinks, the symbols or lights blink continuously at a certain frequency, usually between 6 Hz and 30 Hz. This procedure also leads to VEPs in the EEG, which appear in the same frequency as the stimulus is blinking. A control interface can be implemented using multiple lights blinking with different frequencies, each representing a different command [61].

2.5.3.2 Motor Imagery

Motor imagery is based on the imagination of movements and the corresponding activation of neurons in the specific motor cortex area. These activations happen as a preparation of the movement and are called sensory-motor rhythms (SMR). The subject imagines a certain movement, for instance of the tongue, and an algorithm tries to learn the evoked activation pattern. The EEG channels close to the responsible motor cortex are used.

Increasing activity over a certain brain area is also referred to as 'event-related synchronization' (ERS) and vice versa a decrease in activity is called 'event-related desynchronization (ERD). The patterns intentionally invoked by the subject when imagining movements are therefor called ERD/ERS patterns. The most commonly used frequency bands for motor imagery are the β and μ frequency bands, as defined in section 2.4.2.2.

Motor imagery based BCI systems potentially enable the implementation of intuitive BCI systems. The patterns evoked by the imagination of movement also appear when the subject moves the corresponding body parts intentionally and actively.

Compared to VEP- or SSVEP-based BCI system the motor imagery approach does not rely on stimuli presented to the subject. On the other hand VEP and SSVEP systems involve nearly no training of the subjects. Motor imagery BCI does involve an initial phase of intensive training. Performance and training times differ massively between subjects. Grainman et al. [61] mention a training period of 1 to 4 hours for a BCI system with two commands.

2.5.4 Anesthesia

The measurement of the depth of anesthesia and sedation is another field of application of the EEG. During such states the EEG changes especially in the frequency domain. Examples of algorithms for anesthesia monitoring can be found in section 3.4.3.1.4.

2.5.5 Sleep Medicine

EEG plays a central role in sleep medicine. The medical supervision of sleep is called polysomnography and is largely based on EEG. In section 3.4.3.1.1 the biosignals, the electrode position, standards, and rating criteria of sleep stages in detail.

2.5.6 Other Applications

2.5.6.1 Brain Death

The EEG is used as an additional tool of the diagnosis of brain death, which is an important indicator of death in the legal and medical sense. After brain death the EEG is isoelectric, it only shows a flat line.

The EEG helps to distinguish brain death from states that resemble brain death such as extreme cases of alcohol abuse, overdoses of sedatives or barbiturates, or coma. Nevertheless there are states of profound anesthesia and cardiac arrest that may lead to brain activity undetectable by the EEG.

The EEG is recognized as a diagnostic tool for brain death in several countries, such as the United States of America. The legislation of the United Kingdom does not see it as a

2.5 Applications of the EEG

legally valid tool.

2.5.6.2 Localization of Brain Lesions

An experimental field of EEG usage is the localization of damaged brain areas after accidents or strokes, but also brain tumors can be located.

2.5.6.3 Testing Afferent Pathways

A special application of the EEG is the testing of afferent pathways of the central nervous system. The special wave forms generated by audiovisual stimuli are called evoked potentials, or event related potentials (ERP). ERPs are mentioned in the context of BCI in section 2.5.3.1 and explained in section 3.4.3.1.4, which deals with vigilance and anesthesia measurement.

2.5.6.4 Biofeedback

The Association for Applied Psychophysiology and Biofeedback defines biofeedback as 'a process that enables an individual to learn how to change physiological activity for the purposes of improving health and performance'. EEG as the basis for biofeedback is also called neurofeedback. It is used in the fields of epilepsy, autism [87], attention deficit / hyperactivity disorder (ADHD) [94], sleep disorders [40], and traumatic brain injury rehabilitation [152]. Biofeedback is classified as alternative medicine [87].

Chapter 3

Attention, Vigilance, and Sleepiness

3.1 Introduction

In this chapter we dive deep into the central topic of this thesis: attention, vigilance, and sleepiness.

We start with the definition of several notions that are used in the literature of our field of research. We explain those notions also from a physiological point of view and present processes in the brain that are responsible for their generation.

The modeling of sleepiness and alertness is the next topic in this chapter. We present ways to simulate daytime sleepiness and explain the processes that are the building blocks of the model. These processes can also be measured and estimated by analyzing biosignals.

The various possibilities to quantify vigilance form the major part of this chapter. We describe subjective questionnaires, which help quantifying vigilance, along with several behavior-based methods that estimate the level of vigilance in a more indirect way. The most objective methods are based on physiological parameters. Our special interest are signals that are based on neuronal brain activity.

3.2 Definitions and Physiological Basics

3.2.1 Consciousness and Attention

The term consciousness and attention are closely related. A large number of publications exist trying to define and categorize these two terms. It can be stated that there are two general views on the underlying concept: Some authors see consciousness and alertness as hierarchically dependent processes. Consciousness is seen as a result of selective alertness. Other authors try to explain the two concepts as independent processes, for instance Koch et al. [80] try to show that they are distinct. In their publication they try to show that consciousness can occur together with attention, but also nearly without attention. The other way around, they show that attention can also occur without consciousness. In the following section we want to give some 'classic' definition of the concepts of consciousness and alertness.

3.2.1.1 Consciousness

Conscious perception is produced by cortical processes and activity. The way these processes work are the same in all areas of the cortex. Besides the cortex itself also cortical subsystems are involved in the generation of conscious perception. Examples are the limbic system and the basal ganglia.

Synaptic potentials of the cortical neurons oscillate, are summed up, and synchronized. The intensity and the contents of this activity is dependent on the location of the activity. The actual process, which leads to attention and conscious perception, is the synchronous depolarization of apical dendrites of the cortex.

The distribution of this arousal is realized by a cortico-subcortical system, the limited capacity control system (LCCS). The following areas of the brain are involved in the LCCS:

- the cortex (parietal, prefrontal associative),
- the basal ganglia,
- the reticular and medial thalamus,
- the basal forebrain, and

3.2 Definitions and Physiological Basics

- the mesencephalic formatio reticularis [22].

3.2.1.1.1 Awareness Awareness is a term nearly synonymous to consciousness. Depending on the thematic context the one or the other is used. For example a general anesthesia is defined as a state of unconsciousness, but an unwanted effect during general anesthesia is called 'anesthesia awareness', which is a lack of drug dose to keep the patient unconscious. In the german language both terms translate to 'Bewusstsein'.

3.2.1.2 Attention

Attention can be categorized into general attention and selective attention. One type of attention can change to the other and vice versa. According to the hierarchical approach mentioned in the introduction, conscious perception is only available in selective attention. It requires more neuronal resources in order to lower the threshold of neuronal activation.

A subject needs selective attention in situation which are

- new,
- complex,
- not conclusive, or
- of vital importance.

It is needed to prioritize between concurring aims to control action, to stop following old irrelevant aims (disengagement), to choose a source of sensory information to control action, and to selectively prepare effectors, for instance motor actions [22].

Several parts of the cortex are involved to produce selective attention. The prefrontal cortex is dominant in choosing an aim, the parietal cortex is involved in the disengagement and in analyzing new sensory information, and parts of the basal ganglia, especially the striatum, are important for the choice of reactions.

Lim and Dinges [90] define and categorize attention in a slightly different way. They classify a 'top-down' and a 'bottom-up' type of attention. They see 'top-down' attention as the active focusing on a a relevant event, triggered by a 'knowledge-based' mechanisms. 'Bottom-up' attention is driven by the event itself. This leads to the change of focus.

3.2.2 Vigilance

A large number of publications exist that deal with the measurement of cortical activation and the consequences of an impaired ability to process information. The authors describe these associated states of cortical activation by using terms like 'vigilance', 'alertness', or 'arousal' [111]. Especially 'vigilance' is a term widely used, but also with different meanings depending on the scientific field. In psychology 'vigilance' is categorized as a component of 'attention', besides 'selection' and 'control' [116]. It is described as 'sustained attention', which is the ability to maintain selective attention over time. This type of attention can can be found in watch-keeping activity and is also used by Mackworth [95]. Mackworth invented the famous clock test to measure what he calls 'vigilance decrement' over time.

In this work we use the definition of 'sustained attention', as it is the most common definition in our thematic context.

3.2.2.1 Alertness

Alertness is a term that includes the non-specific activation, or arousal, of parts of the cortex together with cognitive processing. It can be categorized in phasic and tonic alertness, where tonic alertness is synonymous to vigilance [111].

3.2.3 Sleepiness and Fatigue

Weess [164] tries to define and separate the terms sleepiness in contrast to fatigue.

- Sleepiness is seen as a concept that describes the state of wakefulness of a subject. Depending on the situation, sleepiness can result in sleep-onset. Especially monotonous situations can promote the development of sleepiness into sleep, whereas situations of physical or mental stress counteract the sleep onset [110].

3.2 Definitions and Physiological Basics 51

Sleepiness is directly linked to central nervous activation. An elevated level of sleepiness therefore results in an impairment of physical and mental abilities.
- Fatigue describes a psychological state that is dominated by a feeling of exhaustion and excessive demand.

The subject has the impression of a lowered physical power and lowered cognitive capabilities. Disturbed sleep can be a reason for fatigue.

Fatigue may be associated with sleepiness and both states may have the same reasons [110].

3.3 Models and Processes of Sleepiness and Alertness

In 1994 Achermann and Borbély [3] published their ideas about modeling and simulating daytime sleepiness and alertness. Their paper is based on an earlier work of Borbély [25].

In this publication a two process model of sleep-regulation is proposed. One of the model's processes is called C. It represents the circadian rhythm with a period of about 24 hours. The length of the period may vary individually. The other process S is also called the homeostatic process. It represents the sleep debt that builds up during daytime and is removed by sleep, usually during night.

Whereas this model was intended to simulate sleep regulation, Achermann and Borbély extend it with a third process I to make it more suitable for the simulation of daytime. The three processes, and the calculated sleepiness and alertness processes are:

- Process C

    This process represents the circadian rhythm of an individual. An important property of this process is its independence from sleep. It is influenced by an endogenous process with a period of about 24 hours. It works nearly independently of external influences on the organism. This endogenous process is thought to exist in all mammals and has its origin in molecular interactions in each cell.

    The different types of timing are called chronotypes. The terms 'morningness' and eveningness' also describe this phenomenon. External stimuli that influence the circadian rhythm and synchronize it to the environment are called 'zeitgebers' [158].

- Process S

    The homeostatic process is independent of the circadian phase and can be interpreted as 'sleep debt'. This debt starts building up after wake-up and grows with the time spent awake. The sleep debt can only be removed by sleep.

- Process I

    The inertia process I simulates sleep inertia in the positive and negative sense at sleep-onset and after wake-up. Sleep inertia is a state of dizziness and grogginess after waking up and influences mental and physical performance. Reaction times during sleep inertia are directly related to the sleep stage before waking up [65].

- Process AL

3.3 Models and Processes of Sleepiness and Alertness

The alertness process is assembled by the first three processes $AL = (1-S)+C-I$.
- Process SL
  The sleepiness process is also built from the first three processes $SL = S - C + I$.

In figure 3.1 an exemplary simulation of all five processes for two days is shown.

The direct applicability of this simulation of daytime sleepiness and vigilance is discussed in several publications. Åkerstedt et al. [7] discuss its use for the optimal calculation of work schedules in the special work environments of shift workers, soldiers, and railway operators.

3.3.1 Measuring the Circadian Rhythm

Three different aspects of circadian rhythms can be measured.

- The free running period τ is controlled by the endogenous pacemaker. It can be measured in studies by applying a 'forced desynchrony', or a 'free run' protocol [166]. In such a protocol the subject will stay in an environment for several days that is free of zeitgebers, for instance a room without windows and continuously dimmed light.
- The phase angle ϕ is a subject's preferred phase offset to τ.
  The pineal hormone melatonin is a good marker for his phase offset as it is closely related to the light exposure of a subject. A frequently used marked is the 'dim light melatonin onset' (DLMO). Melatonin can be measured by taking a sample of the subject's saliva. Results from subjective questionnaires, such as the Morning-Eveningness Questionnaire (MEQ) have shown a high correlation with actual melatonin measurements. They are often the preferred way of assessing ϕ as they do not require a laboratory for analysis.
  Other markers for ϕ are the core body temperature, the heart rate, and cortisol [166]. Cajochen et al. [34] show in a sleep deprivation study that the core body temperature is a parameter that is only influenced by the subject's circadian rhythm. In their study the high sleep pressure group did not show any differences compared to the low sleep pressure group.
- The amplitude of the circadian rhythm is the third parameter.

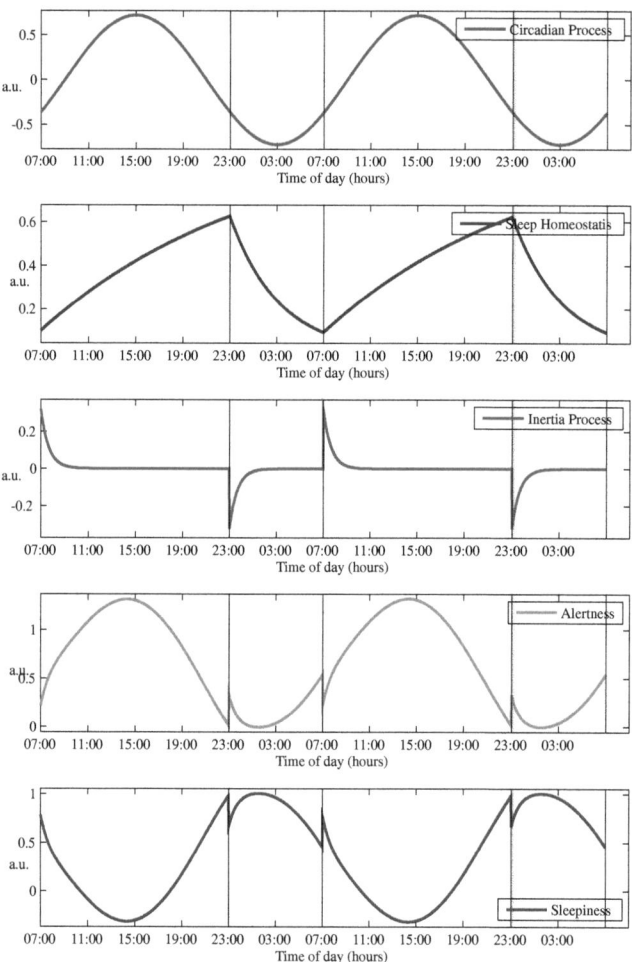

Figure 3.1: This figure shows the three basic processes of Borbély and Achermann's model and the two combined curves simulating alertness and sleepiness. All five graphs cover 48 hours, consisting of two times a day and a night. The black vertical lines represent the begin and end of sleep. The first graph shows an exemplary circadian rhythm. The second graph shows the process S, which represents sleep debt. The third graph shows the inertia process that is relevant before and after sleep. The lower two graphs show the simulated trend of alertness and sleepiness. Their values during night are theoretical.

3.3 Models and Processes of Sleepiness and Alertness 55

There is evidence that controlled light exposure can alter melatonin and body temperature levels [166].

Circadian effects in the electroencephalogram (EEG) are anlyzed since the late 1960ies [73]. Cummings et al. [41] conducted a long-term study in 2000. Their intention was to provide reference data of healthy subjects, which could be used as a control group in pharmaceutical trials. They investigated the EEG of their subjects over 24h, every two hours they recorded for six minutes and analyzed the circadian effects in the data. They found circadian behavior in the theta-band, an alpha-subband (7.0-9.5 Hz), and a beta-subband (12.75 - 18.50 Hz).

3.3.2 Estimating the Circadian Rhythm using Actigraphy

Actigraphy, or actimetry, is the measurement of movements of a subject over a period of time. The resulting in activity patterns are called actigrams. They are used in the analysis of circadian rhythms and sleep-wake behavior. The classic way of recording an actigram is an actigraph, which usually has the form of a wrist watch. This watch-like device is worn on the wrist of the non-dominant arm, which is the left arm in right-handed subjects. The device has to be worn on the non-dominant wrist for at least one week [166].

Artifacts are also an issue in actigraphy. A known problem are subjects that do not wear the actigraph continuously. This might even be necessary in case of non-water proof devices that can not be worn while swimming or showering. The result are periods without recorded activity in the actigram. Those periods have to be recognized as artifacts. Actigraphy is also performed during sleep. The actigram may contain long phases with no activity during sleep. The difficulty in artifact handling is to distinguish between these two kinds of activity free periods.

Technically the central element of an actigraph is an accelerometer, which registers movements in three dimensions. In actigraphy the dimensionality of this information can be reduced, as the direction of movement is not relevant. The number of movements are recorded at a configurable rate (sampling rate) and are saved on a memory chip. After the signal acquisition is finished the recorded movement data is transferred to a computer and is accessible for further processing.

Actigraphy is widely used to measure activity and sleep-wake pattern of subjects. The cosinor analysis is a method to estimate the circadian rhythm based on actigraphy data [13]. The algorithm tries to fit a cosinus wave with a length near 24 hours using a least-squares method. It estimates three parameters:

- the acrophase is the daytime of the maximum of the cosinus wave,
- the amplitude of the wave, and
- the mesor, which defines the mean of the cosinus wave.

An example for an actigram and the result of the cosinor analysis is shown in figure 3.2.

3.3 Models and Processes of Sleepiness and Alertness

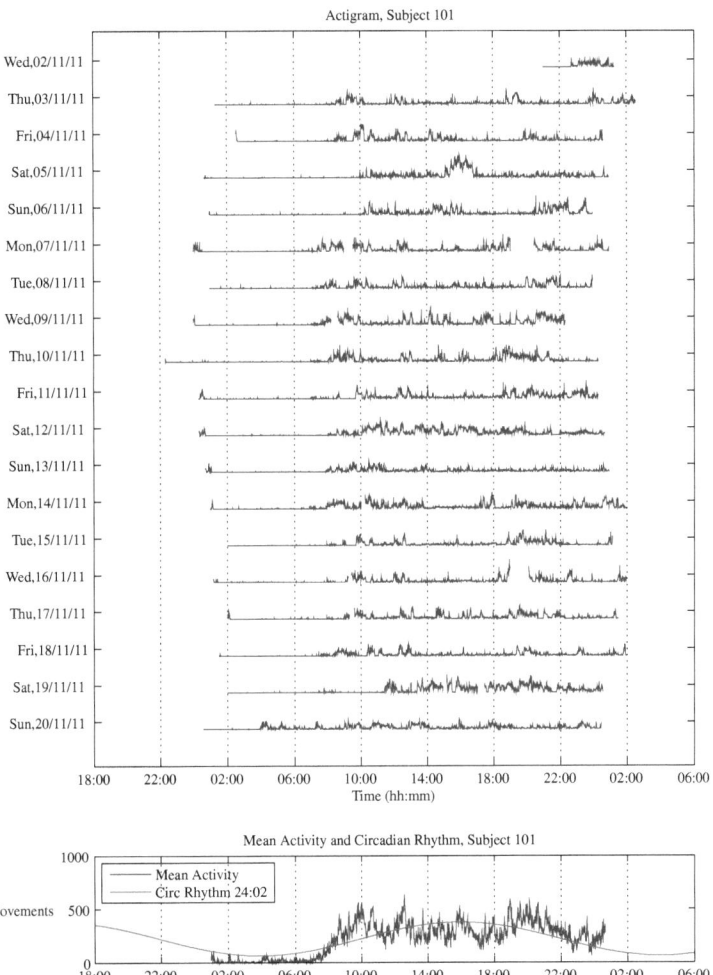

Figure 3.2: In this figure an example of an actigram is shown. The upper part of the figure shows the raw actigraphy measurements over 19 days. The days were separated by subjectively given sleep times. In the lower part of the figure the mean activity over all days is shown. The estimate of the circadian rhythm is superimposed. The rhythm was calculated using the cosinor analysis of the data of all 19 days. A circadian rhythm with a period of 24 hours and 2 minutes had the best fit.

3.4 Quantification of Vigilance

3.4.1 Subjective Quantification

3.4.1.1 Karolinska Sleepiness Scale

The Karolinska Sleepiness Scale (KSS) [8] is a questionnaire that tries to quantify subjective sleepiness. The scale was developed at the Karolinska Institute and is inspired by the Stanford Sleepiness Scale [68], which is described in section 3.4.1.3.

The scale's items were designed following the scaling-method of Thurnstone [153, 110]. The subjective sleepiness is quantified by using nine stages from very awake to extremely sleepy. The subject is instructed to rate its sleepiness during the last ten minutes and to circle the according number. The unnamed stages are also to be used.

1. = very awake
2.
3. = awake
4.
5. = neither awake nor tired
6.
7. = tired, staying awake without problems
8.
9. = very tired, problems to stay awake, fighting sleep

The evaluation of the KSS is straight forward. Values higher than seven mark a high sleepiness, values below four mark the absence of sleepiness.

Several publications discuss the validity of the KSS. Åkerstedt et al. [59] show a consistent and high correlation between physiological data measured in a polysomnography-setup (EEG, EOG, EMG) and the subjectively quantified sleepiness. The high influence of the the circadian process on the subjective sleepiness can clearly be seen in the data published by Cajochen et al. [34]. The data was acquired in a study following a 40-hour protocol with a sleep-deprived group of subjects (high sleep pressure) and a group with

3.4 Quantification of Vigilance

enough sleep (low sleep pressure). Besides the EEG and body-temperature the subjective sleepiness was quantified using the KSS. The results show that for both group the KSS is massively modulated by the circadian rhythm, with a superimposed influence of the sleep pressure.

The KSS was applied in many situations, such as shift work, jet lag, driving abilities, attention and performance, and clinical settings [72]. Kaida shows consistently with Åkerstedt [8] that a rise in alpha- and theta activity in the EEG correlates significantly with the subjective ratings of the KSS. Based on a study with a protocol covering 40 hours Strijkstra et al. [147] draw different conclusion compared to the above mentioned studies. According to them the global alpha activity correlates negatively with subjective sleepiness and only theta-activity shows a positive correlation, especially in the frontal leads. Additionally they give hints on other locally confined correlations of EEG activity with KSS values.

In a real-world driving study Schmidt et al. [136] investigated the relation of subjective sleepiness judgments with physiological measure and reaction times. As physiological parameter they used the EEG-based alpha-event variable of Tietze et al., as explained in section 3.4.3.1.2. The KSS was recorded every 20 minutes. In the monotonous driving situation during daytime they found that the subjective ratings diverged from the other measures after three hours of driving. The alpha-events and the reaction times continued to increase monotonically towards the end of the driving session, the subjective rations follow a U shape. Subjects felt awake at the beginning, started to become tired, and subjectively recovered towards the end of the driving session. The authors are able to show the drivers' misjudgment of sleepiness in driving situations.

3.4.1.2 Epworth Sleepiness Scale

In contrast to the KSS the Epworth Sleepiness Scale (ESS) [56] follows a different approach in subjective sleepiness quantification. Whereas the KSS tries to assess the sleepiness of a subject at the time of questioning, the ESS tries to assess a general condition of the subject. These approaches are reflected in the actual design of the scales.

The ESS measures the propensity to fall asleep in different daily-life situations, such as 'watching television', lying down in the afternoon', or 'in a car while stopped for a few minutes in traffic'. Each of the eight situation has to be rated by the subject on a scale from zero (unlikely to fall asleep) to three (very likely to fall asleep). Re resulting score of 0-24 directly correlates with the general sleepiness of the subject, for instance a score higher than 16 is associated with narcolepsy and other sleep illnesses.

3.4.1.3 Stanford Sleepiness Scale

The Stanford Sleepiness Scale (SSS) was first introduced in 1972 by Hoddes et al. [68]. It is a seven-graded subjective measure of sleepiness. Similar to the KSS, the SSS expresses a level of sleepiness at the moment of the test. The standardized questionnaire contains the following grades:

1. Feeling active and vital; alert; wide awake.
2. Functioning at a high level, but not at peak; able to concentrate.
3. Relaxed; awake; not at full alertness; responsive.
4. A little foggy; not at peak; let down.
5. Fogginess; beginning to lose interest in remaining awake; slowed down.
6. Sleepiness; prefer to be lying down; fighting sleep; woozy.
7. Almost in reverie; sleep onset soon; lost struggle to remain awake.

3.4.2 Quantification of Behavior

3.4.2.1 Reaction-Time and Vigilance Tests

Several approaches exist that try to quantify vigilance based on the the reactions of subjects.

In 1948 Mackworth [95] invented the 'clock-test' intended for pilots of the British Royal Air Force. The pilots were instructed to monitor a watch for two hours. The test of vigilance consisted in the detection of a double-jump of the seconds hand. This test should register the pilot's ability to detect random, rare, and unattended events. Recent versions of the test use a circle of lights or LEDs that light up one after another. The stimulus is represented by the skipping of a light. This vigilance test was also used in a recent study

3.4 Quantification of Vigilance   61

by Hanke et al. [67]. The results from the Mackworth clock test were used as an objective reference of vigilance.

An example for a reaction time-based test is a software designed and implemented by the Siesta Group. The software was already successfully tested and used in the Siesta Project [79]. The software requires a screen and a keyboard. The graphical interface consists of two dark circles, which can turn yellow and red. The subject has to monitor the screen and react to a change of color. Additionally an audio stimulus - a beep - occurres. The correct stimulus is the beep plus the yellow circle plus not the red circle. The subject holds the control-key continuously and releases the key, if the audio-visual stimulus occurs. After pressing the space bar the control key is pressed again as fast as possible. By using this setup it is possible to record the actual reaction time and a movement component of the reaction. The duration of the test can be configured and lies usually between four to five minutes. During this time the subject has to react to a configurable number of stimuli. The average reaction time of all correct reactions to stimuli is taken as the measure of a test. The standard screen and the possible color changes of the circles are displayed in figure 3.3.

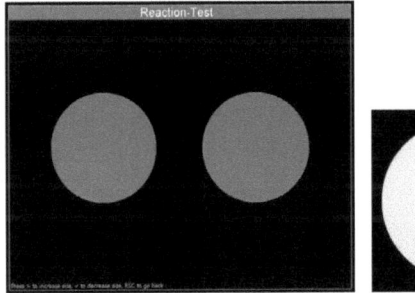

(a) The Reaction Time Test Interface.   (b) The visual stimulus consists of a color change of the circles.

Figure 3.3: The Interface of the reaction time test developed by the Siesta Group. The neutral interface is displayed in the left figure. The possible color changes of the two circles are displayed in the right figure.

3.4.2.2 Psychomotor Vigilance Test

The Psychomotor Vigilance Test (PVT) [90] is a tool that is in use since more than 20 years. The test has become an important way to measure 'vigilant attention' in research involving sleep deprivation. The test has been validated and proven to be 'highly sensitive' [90]. The test is based on a reaction time test with random intervals between the stimuli, usually between two to ten seconds. One test session usually has a duration of ten minutes. During the PVT the subject receives an immediate feedback about its performance. The subject sits in front of a dark screen with a rectangular area. The stimulus consists of the appearance of a millisecond-counter in the middle of the rectangle. By pressing a button the counter can be stopped. Besides the subject's reaction times also false and missed reactions are registered.

To generalize and sum up the major results found by studies using the PVT the following statements can be made: Sleep deprivation leads to longer reaction times and an increased number in missed and false reactions. The 'time-on-task' effect is stronger under sleep deprivation. The results of the PVT under sleep deprivation is modulated by the circadian and homeostatic process, as explained in section 3.3.

3.4.2.3 Multiple Sleep Latency and Maintenance of Wakefulness Tests

An approach to objectively quantify sleepiness is the Multiple Sleep Latency Test (MSLT) [35]. It requires a laboratory environment and is very time consuming and cost intensive. This test currently is seen as the standard in estimating daytime sleepiness.

The MSLT protocol usually consists of five sessions that are conducted throughout the same day. In each session the subject is placed in a light-attenuated and sound-shielded room. Using a polysomnography-like electrode-setup the subject's EEG, EOG, and EMG are measured. The subject is instructed to try to fall asleep as fast as possible. The time between lights-off and the first 30-seconds scored as sleep is calculated.

The tendency to fall asleep and the ability to stay awake are two distinct physiological processes [134]. Whereas the first phenomenon is measured by the MSLT the second is quantified by the Maintenance of Wakefulness Test (MWT) and the Oxford Sleep Resistance Test (OSLER), a simplified version the the MWT[56].

3.4 Quantification of Vigilance 63

The methods mentioned in this section are usually referred to as 'objective quantification'. They all try to measure the time it takes a subject to fall asleep under different conditions. As sleep can be seen as a human behavior [69] we classified these methods as 'quantification of behavior related to vigilance'.

3.4.2.4 Video Analysis

Another attempt to quantify vigilance and sleepiness is the evaluation of facial videos. Some authors [83] try to quantify facial expressions, features of the eyes, and other special behavior by rating videos. Examples for this behavior are nodding, rubbing, or yawning.

Guggisberg et al. [64] investigated the relation of yawning and vigilance. They tested two hypotheses: that yawning is a phenomenon that occurs during drowsiness, and that yawning has an alerting effect. In their study they tested chronically tired subjects, which were placed in a light and sound attenuated room. Besides their yawning-behavior their EEG and ECG was recorded. The authors found evidence that yawning is a sign of decreased vigilance. They were able to show that the delta activity increased before and after yawns. Increased delta activity in the EEG is usually interpreted as a sign of low vigilance and sleepiness. They were not able to validate their second hypothesis stating that yawning has an alerting effect. These results hint that the quantification of yawns based on a facial video can serve as a behavioral vigilance indicator.

3.4.2.5 Special Environments - Vehicle Parameters

A special case of behavioral monitoring is the analysis of vehicle parameters while driving. A driver usually controls several interfaces while driving, such as the steering wheel or the pedals. All of those driver-car interfaces can be monitored and analyzed for signs of sleepiness. This intrinsic approach has the advantage that no additional electrodes or other measuring equipment have to be attached. The driver's state of vigilance can be monitored without performing any additional actions. In this section we present two approaches based on vehicle parameters: the steering wheel, which represents the primary interface of a driver, and the lane deviation [12].

3.4.2.5.1 Steering Wheel The steering wheel angle is a parameter that is analyzed for its sensitivity for changes in vigilance since the 1980ies. Several publications try to evaluate this signal in various ways. One of them is the 'Steering Wheel Reversal Rate' (SRR). This measure counts the number of direction changes per minute. Only movements higher than this value are considered by the algorithm. Values for this threshold range between 0.5 and 10 degrees [12].

Several studies confirm that a vigilant driver steers smoother, with more but smaller movements. A tired driver steers less often and - as a consequence - has to correct the lane deviation with stronger steering movements. To measure this kind of behavior the SRR noise-threshold can be adapted to measure the strong movements. This value is used as a vigilance measure together with the standard deviation of the steering velocity and the steering wheel angle [12].

An example of a raw steering wheel signal, the high-pass filtered signal and the standard deviation of the same signal can be found in figure 3.4. The high-pass filtering is necessary to remove the actual steering required by the road curvature. The higher frequencies represent the steering wheel movements, which are sensitive to vigilance.

Another approach towards the evaluation of the steering wheel signal is the analysis of the signal's frequency domain. Depending on the frequency range analyzed the road curvature has to be known. This is only the case for studies using a driving simulator or in situations, where the driven course is predefined. Gabrielsen et al. published a study analyzing the frequencies between 0.1 and 1 Hz. They found that the Power Spectral Density at 0.45, 0.6, and 0.8 Hz is sensitive to driver drowsiness [58].

3.4.2.5.2 Lane Deviation The tracking of the lane position is an indirect measure of the driver's behavior. A deviation from the marked lane may indicate a high risk for an accident [12]. Camera-based systems can be used for the detection of lane marks. If the car's position relative to the lane border is tracked continuously a value called Time-to-Line-Crossing (TLC) can be calculated. An alarm can be triggered when the distance to the lane border becomes smaller than a defined threshold,[24].

Other authors report a high correlation between subjective sleepiness measures and lane-based parameters, such as the 'lateral lane displacement' or the 'average lane position'. Most of those publications combine these parameters with other measures, such as the

3.4 Quantification of Vigilance   65

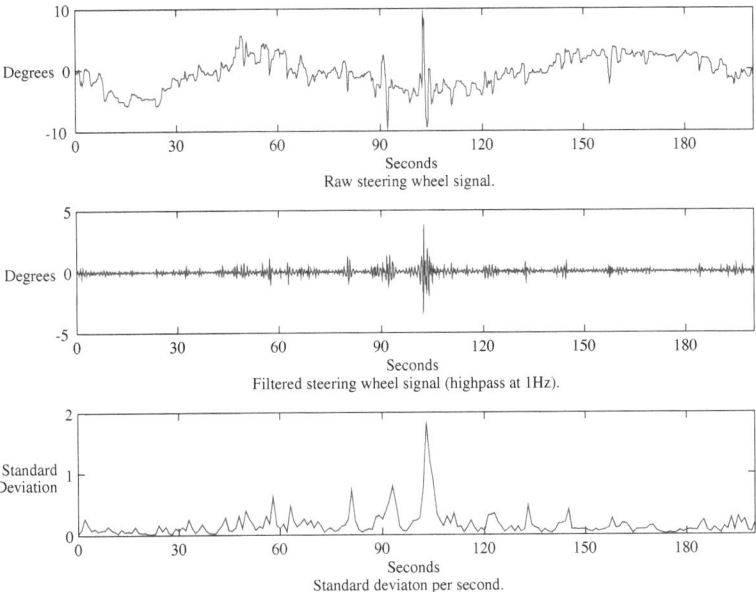

Figure 3.4: This figure consists of three graphs, all three covering the same time timespan of 200 seconds. The first graph shows an example of a raw steering wheel signal. The angle of the steering wheel is displayed, 0 represents the starting position, positive and negative values represent steering to the left and right. The second graph shows the same signal after high-pass filtering. Only frequencies higher than 1Hz stayed in the signal. The information below 1Hz represents the actual steering, which is not of interest. The third graph displays the standard deviation of the filtered signal. The value was calculated per window of one second.

driving wheel angle, or physiological measures such as the eye closure times [125, 12].

3.4.3 Physiological Quantification

3.4.3.1 Electroencephalogram

3.4.3.1.1 Quantification of sleep   The EEG has a long history in being used to assess different states of wakefulness.

For sleep itself Rechtschaffen and Kales (R& K) defined stages in 1968 [129], which mainly rely on EEG signals. These stages are widely accepted and in a version modified by the American Academy of Sleep Medicine (AASM) in 2007 still in clinical use.

A polysomnography for sleep scoring according to the current standard by the AASM is based on the following biosignals [86]:

- EEG data should be recorded using six electrodes at the following positions according to the international 10-20 electrode placement system: F4-M1, C4-M1, and O2-M1. Backup electrodes should be placed at the corresponding positions on the left hemisphere: F3-M2, C3-M2, and O1-M2.
- Eye movements are recorded by using two EOG electrodes. E1-M1 is placed 1 cm below the left eye, and E2-M1 is places 1 cm above the right eye.
- For the EMG recording three electrodes are recommended. The electrodes should be placed relative to the inferior edge of the mandible.

For additional information about the subject's condition during sleep the electrocardiogram (ECG), airflow, and movements of the legs can be recorded. These signals are informational and are not necessary for scoring sleep stages.

There are five AASM sleep stages, which belong to three groups: wakefulness, non-REM sleep, and REM sleep. Non-REM sleep stage three replaces the Rechschaffen and Kales stages three and four [86]. The stages are scored in epochs of 30 seconds. The definitions given here are intended to give a rough overview of the characteristics of each sleep stage. They are only valid for adults and differ for children. The exact definitions can be found in the referenced publications.

- Stage W

  If the epoch does not contain alpha activity but eye activity, such as eye blinks, and voluntary or awake eye movements, the epoch is rated as W. If the eyes are closed and alpha activity is present in more than half of the epoch, the stage is also considered to be W.

- Stage N1

  If more than half of the epoch is dominated by low-amplitude waves in the theta range, the stage is considered to be N1. If alpha activity is not directly visible in the

3.4 Quantification of Vigilance 67

W stage a slowing of the dominant frequency in W of 1 Hz is also sufficient. The onset of N1 can also be marked by slow eye movements (SEM) and vertex sharp waves. SEMs are defined in section 3.4.3.2.

- Stage N2

  The onset of sleep stage N2 is marked by the appearance of sleep spindles and non-arousal K-complexes. An EEG-signal of low amplitude with mixed frequencies is characteristic for N2, together with K-complexes and sleep spindles. The end of N2 is marked by either a form of arousal, for instance a body movement, or by a transition to another sleep stage.

- Stage N3

  An epoch is considered to be N3 if slow wave activity in the delta band is present in the frontal EEG leads for at least 20 % of the epoch. The slow waves usually have a high amplitude of more than 75 μV.

- Stage REM

  The most characteristic feature of REM sleep are the rapid eye movements in the EOG. The EEG stays at a low amplitude with mixed frequencies. The amplitude of the EMG is very low or and must not be higher than in the other stages.

3.4.3.1.2 Quantification of wakefulness In contrast to sleep no standard has yet been established for the quantification of the EEG during wakefulness. In this section we present an overview of ideas and attempts how to quantify vigilance and sleepiness. All of the publications have one feature in common: they rely on a signal analysis in the frequency domain with the purpose to measure vigilance, sleepiness, sleep-onset, or sleep. In the earlier papers the frequency analysis was done in a manual way by evaluating the signal visually in the time domain. The majority of the publications use algorithmic approaches to evaluate the signal's information in the frequency domain. The most commonly used algorithm is the Fast Fourier transform (FFT).

In 1987 Santamaria and Chiappa [135] describe the features of the EEG of drowsiness in adults. Based on a literature review of earlier publications and their own data they classify four stages ('periods') of drowsiness. For these four stages they describe typical EEG patterns. Stages A, B, and C describe the transition from drowsiness to sleep. Stage C already includes early stages of the Rechtschaffen and Kales sleep stage 1 [129]. The fourth stage D describes arousals from drowsiness.

- In stage A, which is called 'transitional period', they describe changes in the alpha distribution on the scalp. They mention the increase of the amplitude of the centro-frontal alpha activity. Their description of changes of the alpha amplitude at posterior leads is ambiguous. For one third of subjects there seems to be a decrease of alpha amplitude during this stage for one quarter of subjects an increase. They also report a slowing of the dominant alpha frequency and a general increase in slow wave activity leading to a mixed pattern of alpha-, theta-, and delta activity in posterior, centro-frontal, occipital, and temporal regions. They describe the phenomenon of burst patterns, including frontocentral sharp bursts and generalized theta bursts. These patterns are only seen in subjects younger than 40 years and are interpreted by the authors as an 'overactive' sleep system and not as epileptogenic activity. A transient phenomenon seen in half of the subjects are negative or diphasic vertex waves. In half of the subjects they report the attenuation of the amplitude of all EEG channels to a value lower than 20 μV for a period of one to four seconds was seen

- Stage B, named 'transitional and post-transitional patterns', describes patterns in a stage between drowsiness and the first R& K sleep stage. Interestingly, frontocentral beta-activity is a significant pattern in this phase. In seven percent of subjects benign epileptiform transients of sleep (BETS) appear during this phase.

- Stage C is the third stage described by Santamaria and Chiappas and is called 'post-transitional patterns'. A general posterior and frontocentral slowing of dominant frequencies is reported as a pattern in this stage. 'Positive occipital sharp transients of sleep' (POSTS) a significant pattern in this stage.

- Stage D describes phenomena happening during arousal from drowsiness. The most prominent of them are centro-frontal beta-activity, vertex similar to those described above, and K-complexes as a reaction of the brain to external stimuli.

Also in 1987 Streitberg et al. described the COMSTAT rule for vigilance classification [146]. Their aim was to describe stages of vigilance analogous to the standards for sleep. Their attempt is based on 'visual patterns' which are variables derived from EEG data. Examples of the 'visual patterns' are the alpha index (AI) describing alpha activity, the K-complex- and sleep-spindle-count (KC and SP), and the background rhythm anteriorization index (BAI), which describes the ratio of alpha- to beta-activity in occipital leads and frontal leads. Based on the 'visual patterns' they describe five different classes. The

3.4 Quantification of Vigilance

features and the authors' interpretation of the five classes are the following:

1. Class 1 describes a state of tense wakefulness with low amounts of theta- and alpha-activity. The anteriorization index is low and if alpha events are present, they have a high frequency.
2. Class 2 is a state of alert attentiveness and has a low amount of theta-activity, a higher amount of alpha activity than class 1 and in some cases a higher anteriorization index than the previous class. The dominant alpha frequency lies in the middle of the alpha band.
3. Class 3 is interpreted as relaxed wakefulness and beginning drowsiness and is characterized by a low amount of theta-activity a high amount of alpha-activity and a high degree of anteriorization. The dominant frequency of the alpha activity is lower than before. Concerning the anteriorization and the alpha slowing the results of Streitberg et al. correspond to the findings of Santamaria and Chiappas, which published their results independently in the same year.
4. The moderate drowsiness-class 4 has a low to medium amount of theta activity and a medium amount of very slow alpha activity.
5. The 5th class, which might already be sleep-stage 1, is called severe drowsiness. Theta activity is high and the remaining alpha activity is slow. The effect of anteriorization is low in this stage.

In several publications a team around professor Åkerstedt at the Karolinska institute in Stockholm analyzes drowsiness in special work-environments, especially those of truck- and train-drivers [17, 60, 160]. In their studies mainly EEG and EOG was recorded and analyzed. The EEG was used as the main parameter for drowsiness, specifically the alpha-theta-frequency-bands. In an early publication [160] alpha activity is seen as an indicator to distinguish a relaxed from a drowsy state. The substitution of alpha by theta-activity is regarded as a further step towards sleep. Together with SEMs, which can be detected in the EOG, the presence of alpha- and theta-activity is used to quantify drowsiness in the Karolinska drowsiness score (KDS) [60]. The biosignals are analyzed in windows of two seconds. If the window contains either SEMs in the EOG or alpha- or theta-activity in the EEG, it is rated with 10 percent-points. If it is free of signs of sleepiness it is rated with 0 points. The ratings of 10 times 2 seconds windows are summed up and form a KDS score between 0 and 100 percent for a 20 seconds window. All available EEG and EOG channels are used for this analysis.

In a later driving-simulator study Annund et al. [17] used the mentioned sleepiness indicators (alpha-theta activity) as an indicator to asses the effects of ruble strips at the edge of a road. Their study clearly shows that the indicators deteriorate before a rumble-strip-hit and sharply improve after the hit of the rumble-strip, which shakes the driving simulator and alerts the driver.

Makeig and Jung set up an exploration study in 1995 [97] to test the relationship of EEG frequency bands with behavior related to drowsiness. The subjects had to react to audio stimuli while sitting in a comfortable chair in a room with dimmed light for half an hour. To induce a monotonous setting the subjects were exposed to a constant white-noise audio-background. The stimulus was a 300 ms rise of the noise amplitude. The authors calculated a task-error rate based on correct reactions to the stimuli and on missing reactions. By smoothing and normalizing they calculated a continuous signal (1.6 s windows) representing the subjects' error probability.

During the experiment EEG channels at Cz and Pz/Oz were recorded. The authors calculated log normalized frequency spectra for 1.6 s windows of each channel. For the time-course of each 0.6 Hz frequency step they calculated a correlation with the task-error rate, which resulted in a correlation spectrum. For all subjects they calculated a mean correlation spectrum. This way Makeig and Jung found a significant correlations at 4-5 Hz (theta-band), at 10-11 Hz (alpha-band) in the Oz/Pz channel, at 14-15 Hz (beta-band, sleep spindle frequency) in the Cz channel, and above 15 Hz in the Pz/Oz channel. The correlations in the theta-band and in the lower beta-band at Cz were positive, the correlations in the alpha-band and the beta-band at Pz/Oz were negative.

In a similar setting [98] they had similar results when analyzing mean spectra grouped by the error rate. For spectra with a high error rate they found a significant increase at 14 Hz, which is the sleep spindle frequency, near 5Hz, which lies in the theta-band, and a significant increase in the delta band. Besides these tonic changes they describe phasic cycles in their data. By applying a second order frequency analysis they found 15-20 s cycles in detection probability. The EEG activity increased at 5Hz before missed stimuli and increased above 35 Hz (gamma-band) before correctly detected stimuli. In a later publication [99] they were able to confirm their findings in more detail. They specified the significant frequency for missed stimuli with 4 Hz and the frequency for correct hits with 40 Hz. They could also confirm a phasic cycle period of 18 s.

3.4 Quantification of Vigilance

The concept of alpha-spindles, also called alpha-events by some authors, appears in several driving-related publications. Heiko Tietze et al. presented the idea of alpha-events at conferences in 2000 [154, 155] and 2001 [156]. At the German Center for Traffic Sciences in Wuerzburg they conducted a driving-simulator study with subjects in awake and drowsy conditions. In a two-dimensional approach they were able to clearly classify the data into drowsy, tired, sleepy, and 'lowered vigilance'. The two dimensions were the length of pauses between the alpha events and the average duration of those events. This EEG-based parameters were compared to a parameter based on the eye-lid closure (see section 3.4.3.2).

The average duration of the alpha events and the duration of average pauses between these events are measured. This reflects the spindle-like appearance of alpha activity in the drowsy EEG. The measure expresses, if the alpha activity is frequent and short or if long periods of continuous alpha activity are present. Using these two values they classify four stages of vigilance: 'wakeful' is characterized by short events and long pauses, 'lowered vigilance' by short events and short pauses, 'tired' as long events and long pauses, and 'sleepy' is defined by long events and short pauses.

Papadelis et al. [114] also connect alpha spindles (which they call bursts of alpha activity) to driving behavior. In a real-world driving study biosignals and the driving behavior were recorded. Alpha spindles increased significantly before the occurrence of driving errors. The driving behavior was also compared to other EEG features, such as synchrony among EEG channels, relative band ratios, and three different entropy measures. Schmidt et al. [136] use a alpha-spindle-index in their monotonous daytime driving study. They are able to show that the alpha-spindles increase over time, along with other physiological measures.

Cajochen et al. [34] from the Center for Chronobiology in Basel, Switzerland, performed a study, where they monitored subjects for 40 hours under controlled condition. Besides core body temperature and the subjective sleepiness they investigated EEG frequency bands. They distinguish 'low activity' between 1 Hz and 7 Hz and 'high activity' between 21 Hz and 25 Hz. They focused on variables that are regulated by the circadian rhythm in contrast to variables that are modulated homeostatically. The latter modulation reflects the time spent awake since the last sleep, as explained in section 3.1. They were able to show that 'frontal low activity' (FLA) of the EEG is mainly influenced by sleep-wake dependent processes and has nearly no circadian modulation.

De Gennaro et al. [43] investigated the changes of EEG frequency components in 1 Hz steps during sleep-onset. They used two different definitions of sleep onset: the first epoch of sleep stage 1 and the onset of sleep stage 2 scored according to Rechtschaffen and Kales [129]. Using principal component analysis they were able to identify four frequency bands that belong to three components. The frequency band from 17 Hz to 28 Hz decreases monotonically during the transition from wakefulness to sleep. This band corresponds to the mid-beta band in traditional terms. The band from 1 Hz to 7 Hz (delta- and theta-band) and from 12 Hz to 16 Hz (very high alpha- and low beta-band) decreases during the transition from wakeful to sleep. The band between 8 Hz and 11 Hz (the low- and mid-alpha-band) shows a U-shape: it decreases during wakefulness until sleep stage 1, stays nearly stable during stage 1, and increases during stage 2.

In the same paper De Gennaro et al. [44] focus for the first time on the micro structure of sleep onset by means of quantitative EEG. The team was able to show that sleep onset can be more reliably described by the start of sleep stage 2 than by the start of sleep stage 1. They compare the mean frequency spectra of 3 and 5 minute periods before and after the defined sleep-onset criterion. They were able to show that before and after the beginning of sleep stage 2 more frequencies change significantly to a higher degree, than in the other condition.

In 2004 De Gennaro et al. [46] investigated the spectral coherence of posterior and anterior EEG leads during sleep-onset. They were able to show an 'information flow' in the delta, theta, and alpha band from occipital regions towards frontal regions during the pre-sleep phase. During sleep-onset itself there was information flow in the other direction in all frequency bands.

Wright and McGown [168] published a paper focusing on airplane pilots in a real-world-setting. During transatlantic flights several biosignals of the pilots were recorded, most notably EOG and EEG signals. Based on these two signals the authors define four stages between alert wakefulness and sleep:

- The first stage is characterized by the predomination of alpha and beta frequencies,
- the second stage shows increased alpha activity and slow eye movements.
- The third stage is characterized by the appearance of theta activity and is defined analogously to the Rechtschaffen and Kales sleep stage 1.
- The fourth stage can already be considered as sleep and contains strong delta and theta activity along with K-complexes. This stage is defined analogously to the

3.4 Quantification of Vigilance

Rechtschaffen and Kales sleep stage 2.

They conclude that EEG and EOG can serve as a basis of objective vigilance monitoring.

Lal et al. [85, 84] use an approach based on the above mentioned stages defined by Santamaria and Chiappa [135]. They band-filter 19 EEG channels in the four classical EEG bands and use a mean value of the values of all 19 channels. The 19 electrodes are placed equally distributed over the crane to cover the whole brain activity. They found that delta and theta activity increases significantly with sleepiness. Alpha and beta activity increased also, but to a lower extent.

Strijkstra et al. [147] investigated the relationship of EEG frequency bands and subjective sleepiness ratings in a 40-hour sleep deprivation study. During the 40 hours the subjects had to rate themselves 21 times on the KSS. The EEG was recorded with the subjects sitting still with closed eyes for three minutes. They found a negative correlation between the alpha power and the subjective ratings, as well as a positive relationship between theta in frontal locations and the subjective ratings. They report a gradual decrease of alpha power with the time awake and an increase of theta and beta power. They take the circadian modulation of all frequency bands into account.

Šušmáková and Krakovská [163] tested the suitability of 85 different measures to distinguish stages of waking, sleep-onset, and deep-sleep. They used a discriminant analysis to quantify their large number of investigated features. The best discriminating features between the stages of conscientiousness were

- ratios of the power of frequency bands, specifically the δ/α, θ/α, δ/σ, δ/β ratios, and
- the relative band power of the δ-band.

Buckelew et al. [30] conducted a study in 2009 and compared a group of subjects with high sleep quality (SQ) to subjects with low SQ. They used the Pittsburgh Sleep Quality Index (PSQI) to assess the quality of sleep. They compared the subject's EEG recordings in four different situations: eyes open, eyes closed, listening to a speaker, and 'high level cognitive flexibility task'. They found significant changes in the theta band. For subjects with high sleep quality the theta activity decreased when moving from the open eyes situation to the listening situation. For the sleepier subjects the opposite was the case, theta activity increased.

Jap et al. [70] also conducted a driving simulator study. They focused in their publication on the relationship of the drivers' sleepiness with EEG-based variables. They investigated the classical EEG frequency bands together with several ratios and combinations of the band measures, such as $(\theta+\alpha)/\beta$, α/β, $(\theta+\alpha)/(\alpha+\beta)$, and θ/β. With the time of driving a decrease of the activity in the alpha- and beta-frequency band was observed. The band-ratio with the highest correlation with time was the $(\theta + \alpha)/\beta$ band combination, which clearly increased over time.

3.4 Quantification of Vigilance

3.4.3.1.3 Other EEG-based methods The concepts presented in section 3.4.3.1.2 rely mainly on the analysis of the classical frequency bands of the EEG. In addition to this approach several authors present ideas and EEG-based approaches to quantify vigilance that rely on other principles.

Pop-Jordanova et al. [124] introduced an index called 'brain-rate'. This index is a 'weighted mean frequency of the EEG spectrum'. They propose it as a brain-parameter analogously to blood pressure, heart-rate, and temperature. In their opinion this value expresses the 'general mental activation level'.

Pal et al. present an interesting concept in their publication from 2008 [113]. They did a driving-simulator study and tested EEG-based measures against the 'driving performance'. Their concepts relies on the setup of an 'alert-model' for each subject at the beginning of the driving session where the subject is assumed to be in an alert state. The following data is expressed as a distance to this initial model ((mahalanobis distance). They find a good correlation between the distance relative to the the initial model based on the theta frequency-band and the driving-performance index.

Entropy Measures In section 2.4.5 we introduced the EEG signal analysis by using complexity measures, such as the Permutation Entropy Index (section 2.4.5.1). Here we present an overview of authors using those measures in their publications.

Olofsen et al. [112] were able to show the applicability of the PEI in the measurement of the depth of anesthesia. They conclude that the PEI could become a simple measure of the anesthetic drug effect for certain drugs.

Bruzzo et al. [29] tried to apply the PEI to the early detection of epileptic seizures. They failed in their aim to predict an epileptic seizure by using the PEI. Nevertheless they were able to show the applicability of the PEI to measure different states of vigilance. They propose the PEI as a measure to classify vigilance states.

The real-world driving study of Papadelis et al. [114] was already mentioned in section 3.4.3.1.2. Besides the frequency-based methods of data analysis mentioned earlier they also evaluated the applicability of entropy measures. They compared the entropy measure to their measure of driving errors. They found two entropies to be the most useful for the indication of driving errors:

EEG Variable	Alertness	Sleepiness	Sleep-onset	Arousal
Beta, general activity	↑ [146, 168]	↓ [97]		↑ [135]
Beta Bursts	↑ [146]	↑ [146]	↑ [146]	
Alpha, general activity		↑ [168,↓ [97]		
Alpha Anteriorization		↑ [135, 146]		
Alpha-Spindles	↓ [156]	↑ [156, 114, 136]	↑ [156]	
Alpha Amplitude		↑↓ [135]		
Alpha Frequency	↑ [146]	↓ [135, 146]	↓ [146]	
Theta, general activity	↓ [107]	↑ [146, 107, 97, 85, 84]	↑ [146, 168]	
Delta, general activity	↓ [107]	↑ [107, 98, 85, 84]	↑ [146, 168]	
Theta Bursts		↑ [135]		
Sleep Spindles		↑ [98]	↑ [146]	
K-Complexes				↑ [135]
Vertex Waves		↑ [135]		↑ [135]
BETS			↑ [135]	
POSTS				↑ [135]

Table 3.1: Summary of the reported trends of EEG features.

This table sums up the publications mentioned in section 3.4.3.1.2. We show the trend of several EEG-based variables on a simplified scale from alertness to sleep-onset and in arousal. The ↑-symbol represents that high values were reported by the authors, the ↓-symbol indicates that low values were reported.

3.4 Quantification of Vigilance

- the Shannon entropy [142] showed a significant decline before driving errors,
- the Kullback-Leibler entropy [62] showed the same behavior, but in a less extreme way.

Blind Source Separation Blind Source Separation (BSS), also called Blind Signal Separation, is an approach to separate the original signals from a number of mixed signals. The approach relies on the assumption that the original signals do not correlate. The approach is called 'blind', because no information about the original signals or the mixing process have to be known in advance. Principal Component Analysis (PCA) and Independent Component Analysis (ICA) are two algorithms that use BSS.

Peiris et al. published a study in 2006, where they try to detect behavioral micro-sleeps in EEG [123]. The subjects had to perform a 'continuous tracking task' while being filmed. The videos were evaluated manually and the detected behavioral micro-sleeps were counted. Several features like the power of frequency bands and ratios of those powers were calculated. To reduce the dimensionality of the resulting feature matrix PCA was used. The principal components were used to classify the EEG data and to build a classifier model. The authors built individual models for each subject and combined all models to a general model. They verified each model by using a n-fold cross validation. They built a mean model for each subject except the test subject and tested the model's performance by feeding the model with the test subject's data. The resulting prediction of micro-sleeps was correlated with the actual micro-sleeps. By repeating this process for each subject the model reached a mean correlation coefficient of about 0.30, which is a rather low value.

Lin et al. [89, 92] make use of PCA in their publication from 2005. They analyzed EEG-data during driving simulator sessions with the aim to classify drowsy and alert EEG data. As a first step they calculated smoothed and log-transformed EEG spectra. The channels were compared to a driving performance index, a measure for the deviation of the vehicle from the center of the virtual driving lane. The best correlating EEG channels were chosen. The frequencies of the EEG spectra of the chosen channels were further reduced by PCA. The resulting principal components were used as input values for a linear regression model. Using such individualized prediction models the authors were able to predict the subject's driving behavior with high accuracy.

A year later Lin et al. [91] proposed a different way of analyzing the EEG data based on the same driving simulator setup. The EEG channels were separated into independent components by ICA. They continued by calculating the power spectra of the independent components in a 1 Hz resolution. A correlation matrix of all ICA's frequency components with the driving behavior was calculated and the best correlating features were chosen by an 'Adaptive Feature Selection Mechanism'. Those were used to train an ANN to predict the driving behavior. The authors were able to build a processing model with a very high accuracy of over 90% in average.

Classification Models Several authors present ideas to classify EEG and other biosignals based on artificial neuronal networks (ANN). The drawback of such a solution is that the discriminating features used by the ANN remain unknown or at least it is very hard to extract this information. In that regard ANN solutions always remain a black box.

Akin et al. [77, 11] chose an ANN-based method to classify EEG and EMG. They use a discrete wavelet transform (DWT) to preprocess the biosignals. The coefficients of the DWT, which represent high- and low-frequency information of the signal, are used as input for the ANN.

Davidson et al. [42] published a study in 2007, where they compare results from a EEG-based ANN classifier to subjects' performance of a visuomotor tracking task. They use 'normalized EEG log-power spectra' as input to their ANN, which they trained using the subjects' performance data. The performance of their ANN was satisfactory.

Gaussian Mixture Models (GMM) are a probability-based approach to classify data. Rosipal et al. [132] use an EEG-based model-approach to classify data of drowsy subjects in a driving simulator study. The EEG and EOG data was rated by experts according to the Karolinska Drowsiness Score (KDS) [60]. For each 4-second window of the EEG a 10-dimension autoregressive model was constructed. The 10 resulting parameters were used as a representation for one window. According to the KDS score windows with high and low drowsiness were chosen. These 'cornerstones' were used to build the GMM, which was designed in an hierarchical way. The authors conclude that regarding performance and computational complexity of their approach are suitable for a 'real-time drowsiness monitoring system'.

3.4 Quantification of Vigilance

3.4.3.1.4 EEG-based Quantification of Vigilance-Related Phenomena The measurement of the depth of anesthesia or the estimation of the brain's 'workload' are phenomena that are closely related to the quantification of sleepiness and vigilance. In this section we present methods and principles to measure such related phenomena.

Depth of Anesthesia Measurement In general anesthesia the unwanted phenomenon of 'anesthesia awareness' is of central importance. During such an incident the patient regains consciousness during an operation, without being able to communicate the situation. This may lead to the sensation of massive pain and may be a traumatizing experience. In order to prevent such situations several EEG-based methods have been developed to measure the depth of anesthesia.

A well-known commercial algorithm is the Aspect Bispectral Index (BIS) [74]. The exact algorithm is not known to the public, but the company promoting the algorithm states that their algorithm is scientifically proven. Contrary to the company's statements there are publications like Schneider et al. 2003 [138], which compared results from the BIS to other techniques that try to assess the state of anesthesia. They conclude that the BIS is not sufficient for monitoring anesthesia. In individual cases the correct classification of patients states was below 70%. Avidan et al. [19] also tested the BIS and draw a drastic conclusion: they explicitly do not recommend the use of the BIS. In a large study with nearly 1000 patients they report at least one case of anesthesia awareness with BIS values clearly indicating a deep anesthesia.

Kumar et al. [82] tested the suitability of 21 different measures to quantify anesthesia depth. In their study they found the following best performing measure: the approximate entropy, the average frequency, the Lempel-Ziv complexity, the δ-, and the β-power. The normalization each value relative to the subject's average value of each measure during wakefulness improved the inter-subject variability.

Tonner et al. [159] investigated the performance of the median frequency (MF) and the spectral edge frequency (SEF) in comparison to the BIS and the Narcotrend algorithm. They compared the values' correctness in different states of anesthesia, such as the loss of response or the loss of eyelash reflex. They found that the commercial systems - BIS and Narcotrend - performed much better than the MF and better than the SEF, which had a prediction probability of better than 80%.

Event-related Potentials Even-related potentials (ERP), also known as evoked potentials (EP), are a phenomenon observable in the EEG. ERP are the measurable result of the brain's response to discrete events [83], for instance sensory inputs to the neural system.

An ERP schematically is a wave with positive and negative peaks called components. The peaks are named P and N depending whether they are positive or negative relative to the signal. Examples for components are N1 or N100, which is a negative peak 80-120 ms after a stimulus, or P3 or P300, which is a positive peak of the wave after 250-600 ms.

The use of ERP in the quantification of alertness is motivated by the observation that during wakefulness, the components of the ERP wave are 'moderate in amplitude, while during slow wave sleep larger responses are visible' [83].

Haenggi et al. [66] use the N100 ERP of an auditory stimulus to measure the depth of anesthesia. Their focus is not the avoidance of anesthesia awareness, but the prevention of unnecessarily deep sedations. They tested the amplitude of the N100 component under the influence of different levels of sedation using several anesthetic drugs. They found that the amplitude correlates with the depth of anesthesia, but is independent of the drug used. They suggest ERP as a supplementary physiological measure during anesthesia.

3.4.3.2 Electrooculogram, Blinks, and Pupils

3.4.3.2.1 Eye Movement A way to measure the movement of the eyes is the electrooculogram (EOG). Either two electrodes are be placed according to the AASM polysomnography setup described in section 3.4.3.1.1, or four electrodes are positioned horizontally and vertically around the eyes. The second approach allows a tracking of the eyes in horizontal and vertical direction.

As the eyes are directly controlled by the central nervous system, the tracking of their movements may serve as an indicator for sleepiness. The relationship of eye movement parameters with vigilance and sleepiness was analyzed by several authors in numerous publications. The two most prominent approaches are slow eye movements and saccades.

- Slow Eye Movements (SEM) are, as the name tells, very slow movements of the eyes with a frequency of 0.1 Hz to 1 Hz and an amplitude of about 100 μV. They appear when a subject is relaxed and during the onset of sleep [160]. In 50

3.4 Quantification of Vigilance 81

% of subjects SEMs are one of the first signs of drowsiness [135, 111] and SEMs are also part of the definition of the AASM definition of sleep stage N1 (see section 3.4.3.1.1).

During the transition from alert wakefulness to sleepiness the eye movements become slower and smaller in amplitude [165]. Atienza et al. [18] finds that for an awake subject SEMs are related negatively to performance and correlate with subjective sleepiness ratings. The Karolinska drowsiness score [60] mentioned in section 3.4.3.1.2 is a measure that is mainly based on SEMs.

- Saccades are very fast movements of the eyes with a peak angular speed of up to 900 degrees/second. When looking around the human eye does not follow continuously but fixates a point and then moves on to the next point. The movements between those fixations are the saccades. The movements are controlled by a neuronal structure called paramedian pontine reticular formation(PPRF). The peak velocity of saccades is not voluntarily controllable and sensitive to sleep deprivation. Zils shows in her thesis
[170] that the peak velocity is a promising parameter to objectively quantify sleepiness.

Hanke et al. [67] compare EOG parameters to results of the Mackworth clocktest. The preliminary results confirm the hypothesis that the peak velocity and the saccade amplitude is negatively correlated to the vigilance test performance.

3.4.3.2.2 Blinks Several authors try to quantify vigilance by observing spontaneous eye blinks.

Caffier et al. [32] use a contact-less measurement system, based on an infrared sensor mounted on an eyeglass frame. They show in their study that several blink-related parameters correlate with subjective sleepiness ratings. They investigated the blink duration, the reopening time of the eye, and the amount of long-closure blinks. They propose their approach as a technology for continuous sleepiness-monitoring.

Oken et al. [111] mention several publications with corresponding results.

The blink rate is another blink-related parameter that is investigated by several authors [111]. The publications are inconsistent whether changes in blink rate are circadian effects or really related to fluctuation in vigilance.

Very fast blinks ('flurries' [111]) might be related to the human self-alerting mechanism and can therefore serve as an indirect marker of the onset of sleepiness.

PERCLOS is a blink-based index intended to measure sleepiness in car drivers. 'PERCLOS is a measure of the proportion of time that the eyes of a subject are closed over a 1-min period as judged by a human scorer.' [48, 12]

A driving simulator study [156] showed a strong correlation between the PERCLOS parameter and driving simulator parameters, such as the standard deviation of the vehicle velocity and the position relative to the lane and several steering-wheel related parameters. The manual visual scoring of eye blinks in videos can be automated by image processing algorithms. This has been shown by several authors [12].

3.4.3.2.3 Pupillometry Pupillometry relies on the effect that the size of the human pupil is controlled by muscles that are connected to the parasympathetic and to the sympathetic nervous system. During drowsiness the parasympathetic tone is dominant and a constriction of the pupil, which is called miosis, can be observed. The sympathetic tone is increased during arousal. This results in mydriasis, the dilation of the pupil. Pupillometry could be a way to objectively quantify alertness and drowsiness [56].

3.4.3.3 Heart Rate

The heart rate variability (HRV) is a measure that expresses fluctuations of the heart rate [12]. Usually the electrocardiogram (ECG) is used as a base signal. An algorithm detects the QRS complexes and the variability of the R-R intervals is calculated. Several publications exist that try to show a relationship between the HRV and the time on task, for instance time driven in case of driver monitoring [83].

Another author [103] discusses the relation of spectral components of the HRV and driving errors.

The results of various authors are not conclusive [12]. The most promising strategies of the HRV analysis is a frequency-based approach, especially the 0.1 Hz component of the HRV.

Sleepiness-related changes in the heart-rate were also reported in literature [111], for instance the decrease during sleep-onset as a consequence of changes in the sympathetic and parasympathetic tone.

3.4 Quantification of Vigilance

3.4.3.4 Electromyogram

The measurement of muscle activity using an EMG is an essential part of polysomnography. The nearly absent EMG signal is a characteristic feature of the REM sleep stage. Several research groups investigate the neuronal mechanisms that are responsible for this significant change of the EMG during sleep [12]. The relation of sleep deprivation and a decrease in the excitability of the motor cortex was investigated by Manganotti et al. in 2001 [101]. They found that the 'motor threshold' and the 'motor excitability' correlate significantly with subjective sleepiness ratings.

Chapter 4

Methods

In this section the methods are described that were used to reach the aim of the objective quantification of daytime vigilance trends using EEG-based variables.

An essential first step was the assessment of the state of the art in the field. The the numerous ideas and approaches from several authors were documented in section 3.4.3.1.2. Based on this overview and the physiological and technological basics presented in chapter 2 new ideas were generated and two hypotheses were derived:

- Variables derived from the analysis of the EEG show daytime trends.
- Variables derived from the analysis of the EEG can be used to distinguish between different levels of vigilance.

A specific study was designed and conducted to provide empirical evidence for the hypotheses. We describe the study design and the subjects, which participated in the study as well as all technologies and methods used in the study: the actigraphy, subjective sleepiness ratings, reaction time tests, and the sleep diary.

The central part of this chapter deals with the artifact handling and the further signal processing. It is focused on the technical details of the different EEG-based variables. Our ideas and successful approaches by other authors were implemented in a processing framework in the software environment 'Matlab' by MathWorks.

The final part of this chapter explains the validation strategies used to evaluate the processed data.

4.1 An Exploratory Study

A specific exploratory study was conducted to provide empirical data to test the validity of the hypotheses and ideas. The aim was to investigate the suitability of EEG-derived variables to measure vigilance objectively on a long-term scale.

26 subjects were recruited and biosignals and other variables were recorded under partially controlled real-world conditions. Two 24-hours recording sessions were conducted consisting of a night and the following day. The sleep-duration differed in the two sessions. Sleep deprivation was induced by instructing the subjects to get up after half of their normal sleep time. Using this setup recordings were acquired of each subject under both conditions.

4.1.1 Design

The biosignals EEG, EOG, and EMG were recorded of each subject two times for 24 hours each. Each session consisted of a night and the following day. During one session the subject had a normal sleep time, the other session took place under sleep deprivation. The subjective normal sleep time was assessed during the recruitment process, where the subjects had to state their average sleep time in the PSQI form (figure A.5). The time of wake-up in the recording session with sleep deprivation was fixed at the time of going to bed plus 50 % of the normal sleep time.

A cross over design was chosen for the study. A randomly selected 50 % of the subjects was chosen to perform the session with sleep-deprivation first and the session with the normal sleep condition afterwards. The remaining subjects accomplished the sessions the other way around.

The study was designed to provide results that have validity in the clinical context as well as in real-world environments. The large majority of studies presented in section 3.4.3.1.2 use EEG biosignals recorded in laboratory environments. This represents a non-realistic environment which may lead to distortions of the results. This issue is especially important regarding the research focus which lies on daytime vigilance trends. A long-term recording of biosignals in a laboratory environment biases the outcomes even stronger than short-term momentary recordings.

4.1 An Exploratory Study

For our study a mobile recording system was chosen that enabled the recording of real-world data. The subjects spent a nearly normal day in their known surrounding, for instance their apartment. Such a less controlled environment induces a broad range of problems, for instance the massive presence of artifacts in the EEG. Nevertheless this way of recording was chosen as it provides data especially targeted at the research focus.

4.1.2 Time Schedule

The two 24h recording sessions took place with an average distance of one week with a minimum of three days and a maximum of two weeks. The minimum was introduced to assure the independence of the two sessions. Especially a precedent sleep deprived session could influence a following normal session.

One week before the first session until the end of the second session the subjects wore an actigraphy wristband and kept a sleep diary. During the time of actigraphy recording the subjects were instructed to keep a regular sleep-wake rhythm, which we defined as going to bed and standing up at the same time every day $\pm$ 30 minutes.
A schematic diagram of the optimal course of events is shown in figure 4.1.

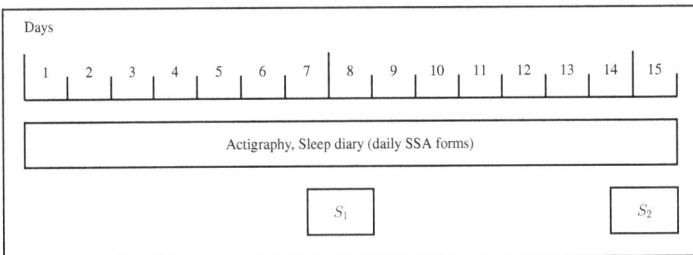

Figure 4.1: The optimal course of events before and during the two recording session S_1 and S_2. Actigraphy and the sleep diary starts one week before S_1 until the end of S_2. The two sessions lie about a week apart.

The subjects spent the nights and days of the recording sessions at home. During the day they were instructed to stay inside a building in a calm environment. In figure 4.2 the proposed time schedule for the subjects' days is shown. This rough schedule served as an orientation for the subjects and was not obligatory.
The subjects kept a log-book and wrote down all major events and activities during the

day.

The subjects were instructed to abstain from alcohol, drugs, and any medication from two days before each session until the end of the recording.

The subjects were following this time schedule, the times given here assume an individual sleep time of 8 hours:

- Day 1 - Evening (22.00)

    - Setting up the EEG-, EOG-, and EMG-Electrodes of the polysomnography recording device.
    - Subjective rating of the vigilance on the Karolinska Sleepiness Scale (KSS) [8].
    - Reaction Time Test (RTT).

- Day 1 - Going to bed. (23.00)
- Day 2 - Morning - Session with sleep deprivation (03.00), Session with normal sleep time (07.00)

    - Completion of the sleep diary form (Self-assessment form of sleep- and wakeup quality).

- Day 2 - Each hour:

    - Subjective rating of vigilance on the KSS.
    - RTT.

- Day 2 - when needed

    - Log-book entry for activities and events.

- Day 2 - Evening (22.00)

    - Demounting of the EEG-, EOG-, and EMG-Electrodes.
    - End of the 24 hours session.

This rough time schedule is also visualized in figure 4.2.

4.1 An Exploratory Study

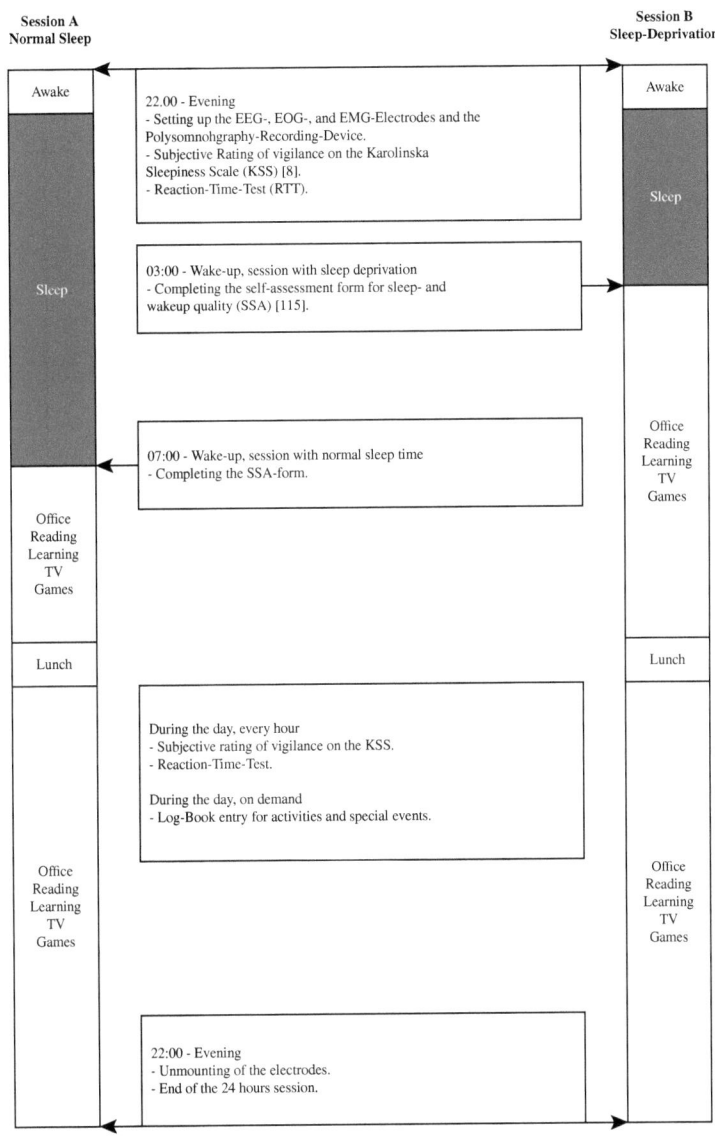

Figure 4.2: The time schedule for the two sessions. On the left side the session with sleep deprivation, on the right side the session with normal sleep.

4.1.3 Subjects

The study aimed to have complete data sets of 20 subjects. Assuming a drop-out rate of 23%, 26 subjects were recruited as study participants. As the study has an exploratory character no formal sample size calculation was performed.

The subjects were healthy volunteers that were recruited via public notices and public postings in social networks like Facebook. All subjects were properly informed and instructed about the study and signed an informed consent form. The text and style of the public notice and the consent form were approved by the ethics committee of the Medical University of Vienna.

The inclusion criteria for the subjects were the following:

- Female and male subjects were included in equal parts.
- Subjects between 20 and 40 years were included. This age group was chosen to reduce known age-specific effects in the EEG [135].

The exclusion criteria for subjects were:

- Subjects with known sleep illnesses were excluded. The Pittsburg sleep quality index (PSQI) [31] was assessed for every subject and had to lie under the value of 6. A questionnaire in German language was used to assess the PSQI, it is depicted in appendix A in figure A.5.
- Subjects with known neurological disorders were excluded.
- Subjects taking medication to regulate high blood pressure.
- Subjects with a regular intake of CNS-active medication.
- Subjects with an irregular sleep-wake rhythm. A regular sleep-wake rhythm was defined as going to bed between 22:00 and 01:00 and having an average sleep duration between six and eight hours. Subjects from some professional groups were therefore excluded, for instance shift workers.
- Subjects with a regular intake of high doses of caffeine (>500 mg caffeine per day [161]) were excluded.

4.1.4 Actigraphy

Actigraphy and its application to estimate circadian rhythm is explained in detail in section 3.3.2.

In the study the subjects wore an actigraph starting one week before the first session until the end of the second session, which was in average 14 days. The time schedule of the study design is visualized in figure 4.1.

The ActiWatch of Cambridge Neurotechnology was used, which is shown in figure 4.3. The subjects' movements were recorded with a sampling rate of 1 sample per minute.

The actigraphy data was used to estimate the subject's individual circadian rhythm. The algorithm to estimate the parameters of the individual circadian rhythm is explained in section 3.3.2.

The actigraphy data during the two session is also used as an additional variable in the data analysis. The signal is called `action` in the following sections.

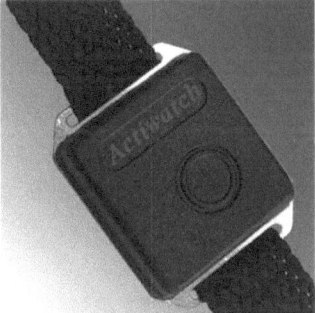

Figure 4.3: The ActiWatch of Cambridge Neurotechnology. The product is now sold by Philips Respironics.

4.1.5 KSS

The subjects rated their sleepiness on the KSS during the whole 24 hours recording sessions - one time before the night and every hour on the following day. The time schedule of the recording sessions is shown in figure 4.2. A basic form was used to note the KSS values in a standardized way. It shows a table with nine rows representing the nine KSS scores and several columns each representing one KSS value. The KSS is explained in detail in section 3.4.1.1.

In the data analysis the KSS is used as a variable at irregular time intervals. The samples' timestamps correspond to the times of assessment as noted by the subjects. The code `kss` was used for the subjective sleepiness in the following sections.

4.1.6 Reaction Time Test

After each KSS self-rating the subjects performed a reaction time test (RTT) with a duration of 4.5 minutes. The RTT software was developed and tested by the Siesta Group and successfully evaluated and used in several published studies. The RTT was performed on standardized laptops.

The RTT is based on a combined visual and auditive stimulus. The test software interface consists of a black screen with two circles (figure 3.3(a)). The visual stimulus consists of a change in color of the two circles. The left circle can turn yellow, the right one red (figure 3.3(b)). The audio stimulus is a loud beep-tone. The subjects have to react to a combination of the two stimuli. The correct combined stimulus is beep - yellow - not red.

The subject has to react to correct stimulus by releasing the control-key of the laptop's keyboard, pressing the space key, and repressing and holding the control-key until the next stimulus. The time between stimulus and control-key release (reaction time) and the time between releasing and pressing the space-key (movement time) is recorded in a log file.

Each reaction time test session has a duration of 4.5 minutes and contains 15 stimuli in a random order mixed with false stimuli. The wrong or non-reactions are also recorded.

Six sparse time series were derived from the hourly reaction time tests and use them as additional variables in the data analysis. The data points of these signals have the timestamp of the beginning of the test.

- `react`: The values of this variable are the mean values of the reaction times of one test session. The timespan between the occurrence of the stimulus and the release of the pressed button was taken as reaction time. Only the correct reactions are counted. The timestamps of each mean value is the beginning of the test.

- `mov`: The variable consists of the mean values of the movement component of the reaction time of one test session. The time between the release of the control-button and the pressing of the space bar after a stimulus was counted as the movement time. The sampling time of each value is the time of the start of the test.
- `fail`: This variable is the number of false reactions per session. The reaction to a non-stimulus was counted as well as a missing reaction to a correct stimulus. The values have the same timestamps as the two other values.

The RTT was designed with the intention to create a monotonous situation. Such a monotony may lead to an increase of false reactions and to higher reaction times. To capture this phenomenon three additional variables were calculated. They are also based on the reaction time,, the movement component, and the number of false and missed reactions, but skip the first 2 minutes of the test session. The values `react2min`, `mov2min`, and `fail2min` cover the remaining 2:30 minutes of the reaction time sessions. The values of the three variables have the same timestamps, which are the beginning of the test plus the offset of 2 minutes.

4.1.7 Sleep Diary

The self-assessment form for sleep- and wakeup-quality (SSA) by Saletu et al. [115] was used as a standardized sleep diary. This questionnaire consists of 20 questions concerning sleep- and wakeup-quality, and the physical condition.

The subjects' forms were evaluated according to a standardized scheme. The result is a number of points per category with values ranging from 7 to 28 for the sleep quality, 8 to 32 for the wakeup quality and 5 to 20 for the physical condition of the subjects after waking up. A smaller numerical value indicates a higher quality. Additionally the questionnaire contains eight questions about the course of sleep, this includes the exact time of going to bed, falling asleep, waking up, getting out of bed, and the number of conscious awakenings during the night. Entering the necessary data takes about two minutes. The test was validated in several studies and can successfully identify subjects with sleep problems.

The subjects were instructed to fill out this form every morning during the time one week before the first recording session until the end of the second recording session, as shown in the time schedule in figure 4.1. The form was used in its German language version and is shown in the appendix in figure A.6.

4.1.8 Log-Book

The subjects were instructed to write down any events relevant to the study in a log-book.

An empty form was provided consisting of a table was with three columns: date, time, event. Examples for events relevant to the study are:

- Eating.
- Drinking, especially alerting or sedating drinks, for instance coffee, tee, or energy drinks.
- The start and end of activities, for instance shopping, going for a walk, or watching TV.

Unfortunately the overall data quality of the log-book entries was very poor. Some subjects wrote several pages of events others only one single line. Because of the enormous variability in the data quality we decided not to use the log-book data any further.

4.1.9 Biosignal Recording

A mobile polysomnography biosignal acquisition device from EMBLA A10 was used in the study. 13 channels were recorded for 24 hours using different sampling rates. 6 EEG channels and the 2 EMG channels were recorded with a sampling rate of 200 Hz, 2 EOG channels with 100 Hz. The sampling rates were chosen based on memory limitations and the duration (24 hours) of the recording. Additionally two EEG reference electrodes were placed at the mastoid positions behind the ears and 1 ground electrode at the front of the subject. The electrode placement scheme corresponds to the recommendation of the American Academy for Sleep Medicine (AASM) for the electrode placement during polysomnography, which is the sleep monitoring in the clinical routine.

4.1 An Exploratory Study

To record the EEG the electrodes were placed according to the international 10-20 electrode placement system [78]. The electrodes were attached manually according to the instructions of Ow et al. [162]. Two frontal EEG channels (F3-A2, F4-A1), two central channels (C3-A2, C4-A1), and two occipital ones (O1-A2, O2-A1) were recorded. The EEG electrode placement scheme is visualized in figure 4.4.

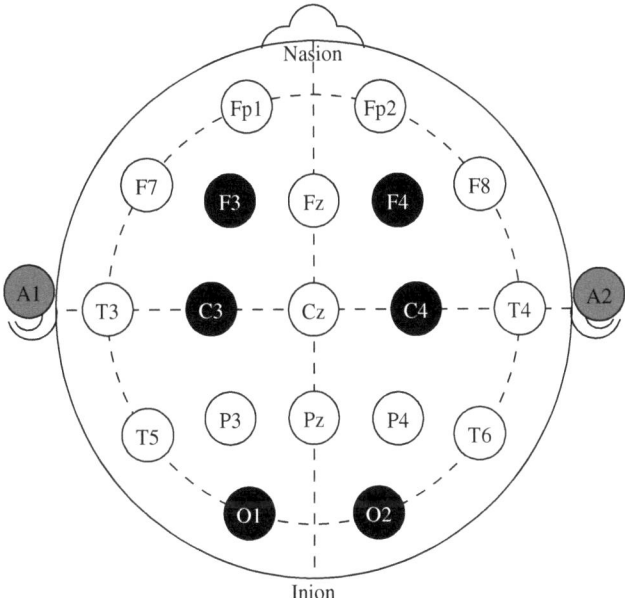

Figure 4.4: The placement of the EEG electrodes according to the international 10-20 electrode placement system.

The electrodes were standard Ag/AgCl electrodes. The skin was prepared using the "Nuprep EEG & ECG Skin Prep Gel" abrasive paste and was cleaned with alcohol. On areas of the skin without hair the electrodes were filled with a conductive gel and fixed using "Fixomull stretch" adhesive stripes. For hairy parts of the skin the electrodes were fixed using "EC2 Genuine Grass Electrode Cream". This paste hardens on contact with air and can be easily removed with water.

Two sub-mental EMG electrodes were attached, as required by the AASM polysmonography standard. Subjects with beards were asked to shave the area below the chin. The two EMG electrodes were placed below the chin with a distance of about 3 cm. The potential difference between these two electrodes was recorded.

Eye movements were recorded by using two EOG electrodes which were place besides the eyes, 1 cm below the left canthus and 1 cm above the right canthus. The EOG signals of both channels was recorded relatively to the A2 reference electrode behind the right ear.

Although mainly intended for the night recordings, the EOG and EMG channels were recorded for the whole 24 hours. Both signals are helpful for artifact detection.

4.1.10 Ethical Consideration

The design and implementation of the study is in full compliance with the Declaration of Helsinki [167].

In full compliance with the ethical guidelines of the Vienna General Hospital (AKH) a vote of the ethical committee of the Medical University of Vienna was requested. A positive vote of the ethical committee without remarks or requirements was received on July 5, 2011 (EK Nr: 622/2011). This document is displayed in the appendix in figures A.1 and A.2.

4.1.11 Data Security and Subject Privacy

An identification number was assigned to each subject. The data analysis happened in a completely pseudonymized way. Only authorized persons had access to the personalized raw data. The data was stored in a secure way and is only accessible to authorized persons.

The subjects were informed about this procedure and were assured that their personal information, such as their names, will never be published in any way.

4.1.12 Risk-Benefit Analysis

The subjects did not have any direct advantage in participating in the study, which was clearly communicated in the informed consent form.

During one recording session the subjects were exposed to sleep deprivation. To prevent problems or incidents because of the induced sleep deprivation the subjects were

4.1 An Exploratory Study

instructed not to drive or operate big machines during this session. To further reduce any risk the session with sleep deprivation were scheduled on days where the subjects could stay at home, for instance weekends or holidays.

The potential risk of disclosure of sensitive subject data was reduced by pseudonymizing the data and restricting data access.

4.2 EEG Artifact Handling

Artifacts are an issue that can never be ignored in biosignals. The possible types of artifacts that can be present in the EEG are described in section 2.4.1.

The detection and removal of artifacts was explicitly not a focus of this thesis. The project was a cooperation with the company Siesta Group, which are the originators of the automatic sleep scoring software Somnolyzer 24x7. The main purpose of the software is to process biosignals of the EEG, EOG, and EMG which were recorded during polysomnography. The Somnolyzer 24x7 algorithm is able to classify sleep stages with the same accuracy as trained human raters [15].

The Somnolyzer 24x7 software is intended to be used with raw biosignals. It therefore includes a biosignal preprocessing, which detects and marks artifacts. This analysis additionally uses the EMG and EOG channels to optimally detect and classify artifacts in the EEG signal. The Siesta Group analyzed the biosignal data using the Somnolyzer 24x7 algorithm and provided the signal annotation.

In figure 4.5 the preprocessing of the EEG data is illustrated. As explained in section 4.1.9 two frontal, two central, and two occipital referential EEG channels were recorded. The two channels were recorded from a position on the left hemisphere and the mirrored position on the right hemisphere. The Somnolyzer 24x7 software provides a quality based choice of the two channels at each position. According to this quality information mixed channels for the three recording positions were assembled, which contain the parts of the signal with the best recording quality.

The resulting mixed signal still contains artifacts. The Somnolyzer 24x7 algorithm is able to distinguish between 11 different artifact types. In figure 4.5 the procedure of marking the windows that contain any type of artifact is shown schematically. Following this procedure fragmented but artifact free signals were created. These signals are the basis of the further EEG processing.

The Somnolyzer 24x7 algorithm detects 10 different types of artifacts. The codes starting with art- are the abbreviations used in the following sections.

1. No power (art-no-power): The signal's spectral frequency power of the window is zero.

4.2 EEG Artifact Handling

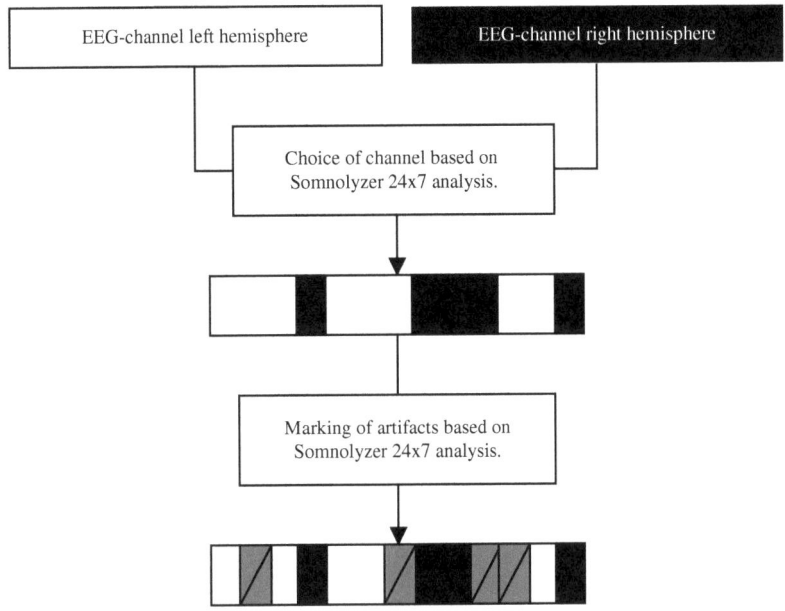

Figure 4.5: Each of the three EEG positions is recorded using two electrodes, one on the left and one on mirrored position on the right hemisphere. The two channels are mixed together based on the quality analysis of the Somnolyzer 24x7 algorithm. The artifacts of the resulting mixed signal are marked. The result is a mixed, fragmented, and artifact-free EEG signal.

2. No variance (`art-no-variance`): The variance of the signal window is zero.
3. Amplitude (`art-amplitude`): The signal contains amplitude values, which are physiologically not plausible.
4. Absolute low frequencies (`art-low-abs`): The signal contains very low frequencies. This may indicate moving electrodes, for instance as a result of sweating.
5. Relative low frequencies (`art-low-rel`): The signal contains low frequencies in relation to the rest of the signal. These frequencies are too low to plausibly originate from the brain.
6. Absolute high frequencies (`art-high-abs`): The signal contains very high frequencies. This are most likely artifacts resulting from muscle activity.

7. Relative high frequencies (art-high-rel): Relative to the rest of the signal the current window has high frequency components. These frequencies are too high to have their origin in the EEG.
8. EOG (art-eog): The analyzed section of the signal contains EOG artifacts, as explained in section 2.4.1. This includes any kind of eye activity, for instance blinks, slow and fast eye movements.
9. Synchronization right (art-sync-r): This artifact type indicates a problem in the synchronicity of the right channel.
10. Synchronization left (art-sync-l): This artifact type indicates a problem in the synchronicity of the left channel.

The fraction of artifacts in the data is 57.24 % for all recorded samples during wakefulness, 60.4 % on the days after normal sleep and 54.72 % for the recorded samples during sleep-deprivation.

Table 4.1 gives an overview of the fraction of artifact types relative to detected artifacts. The largest fraction of artifacts is resulting from muscle activity (art-high-abs) with 48.55 % of all detected artifacts. The second largest fraction is caused by eye movements (art-eog) and accounts for 36.01 % of all artifacts during wakefulness.

Artifact Type	All sessions	Normal sessions	Sleep Deprived sessions
art-high-abs	0.4855	0.5043	0.4690
art-eog	0.3601	0.3381	0.3795
art-high-rel	0.1067	0.1079	0.1057
art-sync-l	0.0465	0.0484	0.0448
art-amplitude	0.0004	0.0006	0.0003
art-no-variance	0.0004	0.0003	0.0005
art-low-abs	0.0002	0.0002	0.0002
art-low-rel	0.0001	0.0001	0.0001
art-no-power	0.0000	0.0000	0.0000
art-sync-r	0.0000	0.0000	0.0000

Table 4.1: The fraction of artifact types relative to all artifacts. The values are give for all samples during wakefulness for data during sessions after normal sleep and for the sleep deprived wakefulness.

4.2.1 Artifact-based Variables

The idea of using EEG artifacts as meaningful variables is a novelty in the analysis of the EEG during wakefulness. Usually artifacts are seen as an obstacle to EEG processing, especially during wakefulness under not completely controlled conditions. Nevertheless it is crucial for the approach to clearly distinguish between artifact free EEG and the parts of the EEG, which are influenced by any kind of artifacts. Based on the Somnolyzer 24x7 analysis 10 binary artifact signals were generated. Additionally an eleventh binary artifact signal (`art_general`) was calculated that indicates the presence of artifacts of any kind.

The binary artifact signals are adapted to a 2 seconds window size by calculating the mean value of the artifact signal in the window. The result is a time series with values between 0 and 1.
1 corresponds to a window, which is completely filled with artifacts of one type.

4.3 EEG-based Variables

4.3.1 Frequency-band-based Variables

The frequency-based analysis of EEG signals is the most common way of EEG processing. It is also widely used in literature, as shown in the literature analysis in section 3.4.3.1.2. The mathematical background of the analysis of signals in the frequency domain is presented in section 2.4.2.

At this point the exact algorithm used to analyze the signal in the frequency domain is documented. The algorithm is based on the short-time Fourier transform (STFT), which is a transform similar to the classical Fourier transform defined in section 2.4.2. 1 second windows were used for the STFT with 50% overlap and instructed the function to analyze the frequencies between 1 Hz and 100 Hz under consideration of the Nyquist theorem (section 2.3.2.1)and the EEG sampling rate of 200 Hz. The Matlab implementation in the function `spectrogram` was used for the calculations.

Power Spectral Density One of the results of the `spectrogram` function is the power spectral density (PSD) of each window and for every frequency in Hz. To calculate the PSD of a frequency band for a window a mean PSD of all frequencies in the frequency band was used. In the software framework a general windows size of 2 seconds was used. To have a result vector which corresponds to a sampling rate of 1 sample per 2 seconds the mean of every frequency band PSD values of all spectrogram-windows within the 2 seconds window was calculated.

In the implementation the cut-off frequencies defined in table 4.2 were used to confine the EEG frequency bands. The abbreviations in this table are the same as the ones use the figures and following tables in this section.

Relative PSD Besides the absolute PSD values the relative PSD values for the classical EEG bands were calculated, which are defined in the leftmost column of table 4.2. For each window the PSD values of the delta, theta, alpha, beta, and gamma band were summed up and this sum was used to normalize the absolute PSD values. For example the relative beta PSD was calculated as

4.3 EEG-based Variables

delta 01.00 03.90			
theta 04.00 07.90			
alpha 8.00 13.90	alpha1 8.00 10.90	alpha2 11.00 13.90	
beta 14.00 29.90	beta1 14.00 19.29	beta2 19.30 24.59	beta3 14.60 29.90
gamma 30.00 49.90	gamma1 30.00 39.90	gamma2 40.00 49.90	

Table 4.2: The definition of the EEG frequency bands as they were used in the Matlab implementation.

$$\beta_r = \frac{\beta}{\delta + \theta + \alpha + \beta + \gamma},$$

where the Greek letters without index stand for the absolute PSD value.

The following abbreviations were used for these variables: `delta_r`, `theta_r`, `alpha_r`, and `beta_r`, `gamma_r`.

Frequency band ratios It is known from literature (section 3.4.3.1.2) that some ratios of the frequency bands are sensitive to changes in vigilance. The two most promising frequency band ratios were used and implemented:

- α/θ frequency band ratio (`alpha_theta`), and the
- $(\theta + \alpha)/\beta$ combination of frequency bands (`theta_alpha_beta`), which was found useful by Jap et al. [70].

4.3.2 Amplitude-based Variables

Kurtosis The kurtosis value of the EEG signal was calculated for every window as defined in section 2.4.4. The resulting variable is called `kurtosis`.

Standard Deviation A number of variables were calculated based on the standard deviation, as explained in section 2.4.4. The EEG signal was filtered using the band limits in table 4.2 and calculated the standard deviation from the resulting band-filtered signal in the time domain.

The variables are called according to the band-names in table 4.2 plus the suffix `_std`.

4.3.3 Complexity-based Variables

One of the exploratory approaches is the use of complexity measures (section 2.4.5) to describe changes in the EEG signals. The Permutation Entropy Index (`pei`) was implemented as is explained in section 2.4.5.1.

4.3.4 Event-based Variables

Mean event duration and pauses The idea of using the duration of events and the duration of the pauses between them as variables is partly explained in sections 2.4.4 and 3.4.3.1.2. At this point an exact definition of the algorithms is given. The concept of events was implemented for the alpha and the theta frequency band.

As the basis of the algorithm the absolute values of the bandpass-filtered raw EEG data are used

$$X = abs(filter_{bandpass}(data_{raw})) = x_1, x_2, ..., x_n.$$

Based on this time series a statistical threshold is calculated [155]

$$threshold = mean(X) * 2.$$

All data points greater or equal than the threshold are declared as events, and all other data points as pauses. This way two binary signals are defined as

$$Event = e_1, e_2, ..., e_n \text{ with } e_i = \begin{cases} 1 & x_i \geq threshold \\ 0 & x_i < threshold \end{cases}$$

and

4.3 EEG-based Variables

$$Pause = p_1, p_2, ..., p_n \text{ with } p_i = \begin{cases} 0 & x_i \geq threshold \\ 1 & x_i < threshold \end{cases}.$$

The final step of the implementation calculates the mean duration of the events ($DEevent$) of each window and the mean duration of the pauses ($DPause$). The standard windows size is $win = 2s$, which leads to a number of $m = n/win$ windows. First the number of state changes of the events is counted

$$CEvent = ce_1, ce_2, ..., ce_{n-1} \text{ with } ce_i = e_{i+1} - e_i, \text{ and the pauses}$$

$$CPause = cp_1, cp_2, ..., cp_{n-1} \text{ with } cp_i = p_{i+1} - p_i.$$

The maximum of the positive and negative changes in a window from $w_{min} = (j-1) * win + 1$ to $w_{max} = j * win$ is calculated.

$$change_j = max(\sum_{k=w_{min}}^{w_{max}} (ce_k > 0), \sum_{k=w_{min}}^{w_{max}} (ce_k < 0)),$$

where $ce_k > 0$ and $ce_k < 0$ stand for logical functions, which have a binary result resulting from the condition.

And finally the actual mean durations are defined as

$$DEvent = de_1, de_2, ..., de_m \text{ with } de_j = \sum_{k=w_{min}}^{w_{max}} e_k/change_j, \text{ and}$$

$$DPause = dp_1, dp_2, ..., dp_m \text{ with } dp_j = \sum_{k=w_{min}}^{w_{max}} p_k/change_j.$$

Additionally the factor of the two values is calculated:

$$DFactor = \frac{DEvent}{DPause}$$

In the following sections these three values for the alpha frequency band are called `alpha_event`, `alpha_pause`, and `alpha_factor`, and for the theta frequency band `theta_event`, `theta_pause`, and `theta_factor`.

Sleep Spindles Sleep spindles are a transient phenomenon, which typically appears in the EEG during the Rechtschaffen and Kales sleep stage 2 (section 3.4.3.1.2). According to several publication such as Anderer et al. [16] the origin of the spindles lies in the thalamus. These spindles have frequencies between 7 Hz and 14 Hz.

As explained in the section about artifact handling (4.2), we used the Somnolyzer algorithm to analyze the data. The main purpose of this was the detection of artifacts. As a side-effect the algorithm - actually intended for EEG during sleep - also analyzed several other variables. One of them are the sleep spindles, which are essential to recognize the sleep stage 2.

In the following sections the variable describing the detected sleep spindles during the course of the daytime recording is called `spindles`.

4.3.5 Spectral Variables

The Spectral Edge Frequency (SEF) is a measure based on the frequency spectrum of a signal. The SEF is based on the area under the curve of the spectrum. It is defined as the frequency f, which marks the limit, where n percent of the area under the curve lie. The concept is shown in figure 4.6.

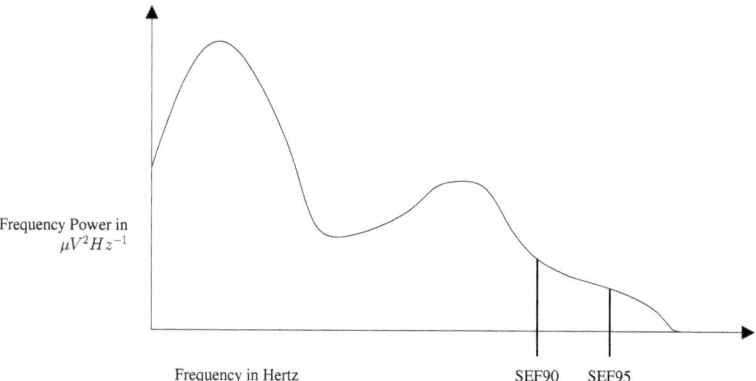

Figure 4.6: The schematic concept of the spectral edge frequency. The area left of the SEF90 and SEF95 represent 90% and 95% of the area under the spectral curve.

4.4 Analysis of the Data

20 complete data sets were successfully acquired, which is an equivalent of about 960 hours of recorded biosignals. The analysis of this thesis is focused on the biosignals during wakefulness.

The study was designed with the intention to record the biosignals under realistic and real-world conditions. This idea was implemented by instructing the subjects to spend the day of the recording session in their apartments and to their activities to office work and to avoid physical activities, for instance sports. It was already clear to us during the design phase that these instructions are very vague and will not be sufficient to record artifact free biosignals. As a consequence 57.24 % of all recorded data during wakefulness were artifacts. A basic statistical overview of the frequency and distribution of artifacts in the recorded data is presented in table 4.1.

For any further EEG analysis only artifact free sections of the biosignals were used based on the artifact handling explained in figure 4.5. The removal of artifacts by filtering and other means was considered, but we decided to stick to clearly artifacts free EEG to avoid signal distortions and possibly misleading results.

The consequence are very fragmented EEG signals. An example of an EEG variable of one subject is shown in its raw form in figure 4.7. The fragmentation because of artifacts and the strong fluctuations of the raw data can be clearly seen. The data is shown relative to the time of waking up, therefore the data of the normal day on the left side in red is shorter than the day under sleep deprivation, which is shown on the right side in blue. The time is normalized to a scale between 0 and 1, where 1 represents 24 hours.

Before analyzing any trends in this data it was aggregated in slices. The data was analyzed relative to different time scales such as the time since waking up or the circadian phase. Therefore the data was aggregated according to a general procedure: each slice represents 5 % of the whole time-range. The analysis of data relative to the time of waking up, where 1 represents 24 hours and one slice of 5 % (0.05) covers 1.2 hours.

The aggregation of data points within a time slice overcomes the problem of fragmented data. The median value of all data points was used as a means of aggregation. In figure 4.8 the aggregation of the data from figure 4.7 is shown in the described way. The time series of medians for the normal session of this example subject is shown on the left in

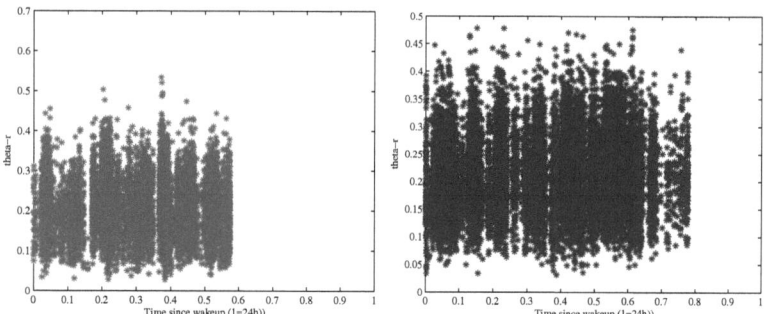

Figure 4.7: Example of a raw fragmented EEG variable.

red, the median time series under the sleep deprived condition is shown in blue on the right.

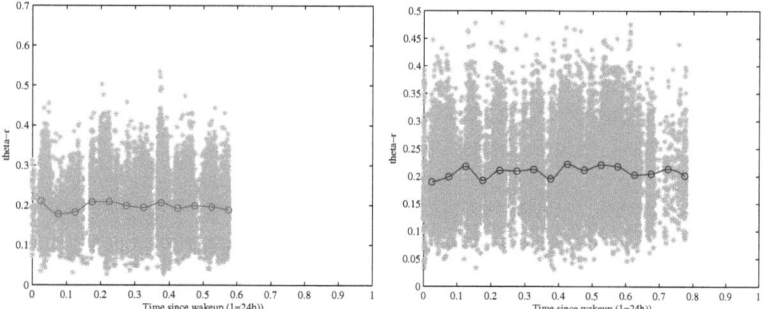

Figure 4.8: Example of the aggregation of the raw EEG data using the median values per slice.

In general the EEG and its derived parameters show intra- and inter-subject variability. This means that multiple recordings of the same subject under the same conditions may lead to different nominal values. The same is true for recordings of different subject under the same conditions. Several publications investigate which kind of EEG-based variable are more affected by this phenomenon than others [63, 39].

The focus in the analysis of EEG is the daytime trend of EEG-based variables. Therefore the absolute values were not of interest, but their course over time. To circumvent unwanted effects due to intra- and inter-subject variabilities a normalization of the data was introduced. Each recorded session was normalized relative to the first time slice. Each of

4.4 Analysis of the Data

the daytime trend curves starts with the nominal value of 1 and develops relatively to this over the day. The normalization of the aggregated data from figure 4.8 is visualized in 4.9. The normal session data and the data from the sleep deprived session are visualized in the same figure.

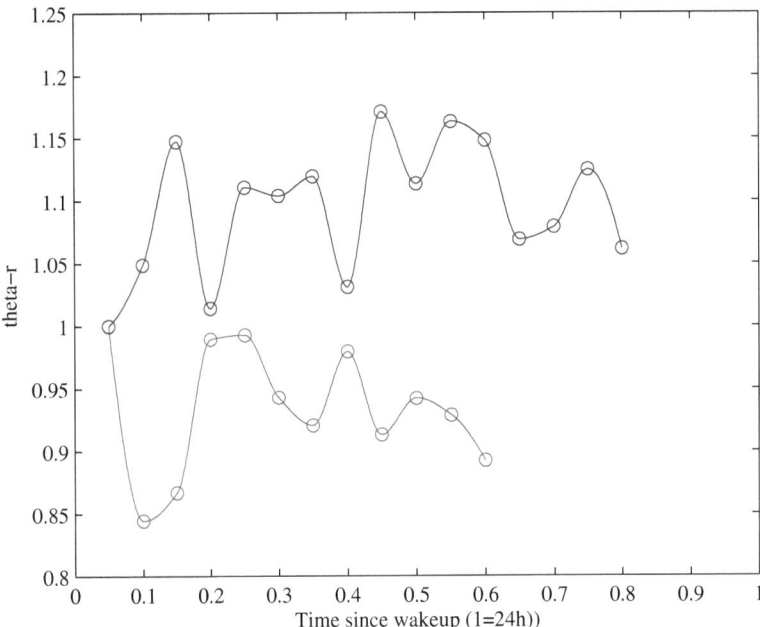

Figure 4.9: Example of a normalized aggregated trend of an EEG-based variable.

Based on the aggregated and normalized daytime trends of the variables it is possible to compare the sessions and subjects. To make statistical statements about general trends in the data the subject's data was further aggregated to a generalized model. The data of all valid time slices of the subjects' individual daytime curves are aggregated by calculating the median of all valid sessions per time-slice. Time slices with less than 2 data points were skipped. The procedure is visualized in figure 4.10. The circles in red represent the individual values of the subject's normal daytime values, the blue circles the individual sleep deprived data points. The continuous curve is the calculated median for the normal sessions (red) and the sleep deprived sessions (blue).

110   Methods

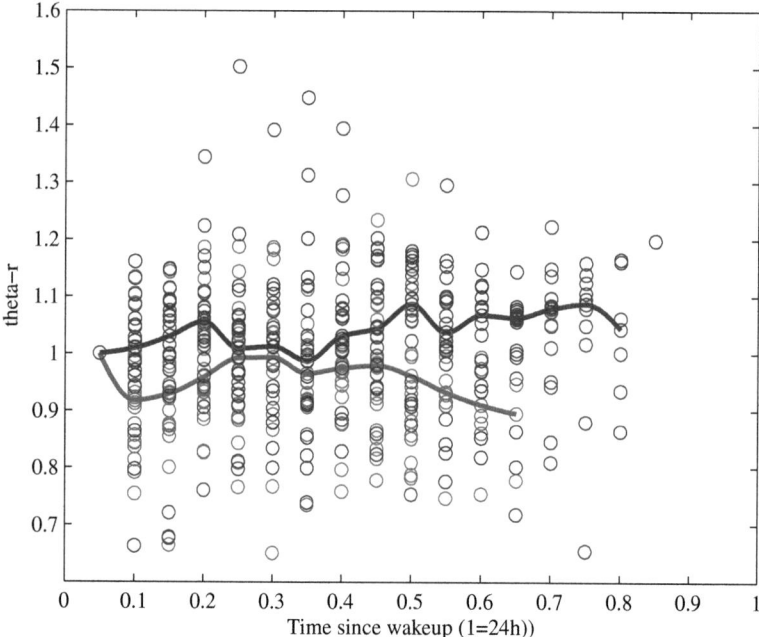

Figure 4.10: Example of the aggregation of individual daytime trends to a general model.

4.5 Validation Strategies

In the introduction of this chapter two hypotheses were formulated. The aim is to validate the hypotheses by providing empirical evidence based on the data acquired in the study.

The first hypothesis assumes that the EEG-based variables show daytime trends. The variables' relationship with different time scales are analyzed. The validation strategy to prove this hypothesis is based on the 3-process model presented by Achermann and Borbély [3], which is explained in detail in section 3.3. This model is built on basic processes like the homeostatic process and the circadian process. Empirical evidence is given that EEG-derived variables correspond with these processes during wakefulness as well as with the 3-process model itself.

4.5.1 Homeostatic Properties

Achermann and Borbély's homeostatic process describes the concept of sleep debt, which accumulates during wakefulness and is compensated by sleep. In order to find variables, which correspond to this idea during wakefulness, the time since wake-up is used as the timescale. This timescale is normalized to a value range of 0 to 1, where 1 stands for 24 hours.

The homeostatic process of the model behaves in a nearly linear way. To show such a behavior of a variable it is necessary to find evidence for a linear trend of the variable with the chosen time scale.

The Kendall τ rank correlation coefficient [75] is a measure, which exactly fulfills this purpose. A rank correlation coefficient is a non-parametric measure for the correlation of two variables. It measures the monotonous linear relation without assuming a special probability distribution of the variables. Kendall's τ is based on the comparison of pairs of values (x_i, y_i) and (x_j, y_j), which are sorted by one of the two variables, for instance x. The indices are $i = 1, ..., n-1$ and $j = i+1$ and $x_1 \leq x_2 \leq ... \leq x_n$.

The calculation of τ is based on counting the number of pairs which fulfill a number of criteria:

- C stands for the number of pairs, where $x_i < x_j$ and $y_i < y_j$ is true.

- D is the number for pairs with $x_i < x_j$ and $y_i > y_j$.
- T_Y is the count of pairs with $x_i <> x_j$ and $y_i = y_j$.
- T_X counts the number of pairs with $x_i = x_j$ and $y_i <> y_j$.

Based on these counts, Kendall's τ is defined as

$$\tau = \frac{C - D}{\sqrt{(C + D + T_X) * (C + D + T_Y)}}.$$

The nominal value of τ lies in the range of $-1 \leq \tau \leq 1$. A negative τ indicates a negative correlation of the two variables, a positive value stands for a positive correlation.

If the two variables are completely independent τ will be zero, which is also the null hypothesis for the significance test. If it is rejected by a value lower than 5 %, the two variables are considered to be significantly dependent.

4.5.2 Circadian Properties

The circadian process is the second process described by Achermann and Borbély. It directly influences the model of daytime alertness and sleepiness. The properties of this process are described in detail in section 3.3. Actigraphy is used to estimate the circadian rhythm, especially its length and its phase relative to the daytime. The circadian rhythm estimated from actigraphy has a daytime offset comparable to the rhythm of the core body temperature.

The analysis of EEG-based variables that behave in a circadian way is based on this estimation. The variables' timescale is adapted to fit the individual circadian rhythm. For the circadian phase a scale from 0 to 1 is used. 0 represents the minimal amplitude of the actigraphy based estimate of the circadian rhythm on the day of measurement, and 1 represents the next minimum, which is in average 24h later. The actual duration of the circadian period varies by subject between 23 and 25 hours.

Again, the subject's data is aggregated in time slices by using the median value. One slice covers 5 % of the possible value range of the circadian phase, which leads to 20 slices covering the whole circadian period. The same principle of data normalization and aggregation is used as for the evaluation of homeostatic trends. The median value of the first time slice is used as normalizing factor for a sessions's time series of data points.

4.5 Validation Strategies

This way the subjective sessions become comparable with each other.

A property of circadian behavior is the independence of sleep and sleep pressure. As a consequence it can be ignored, whether a session was recorded under sleep deprivation or after normal sleep. The circadian trends will or will not be present at the same extent. To come to a statistical conclusion all session's data was aggregated by using median values per time slice, following the principle visualized for homeostatic trends in figure 4.10. The result is a circadian model of a variable covering all subjects.

To evaluate the fit of the EEG-based variables to describe a circadian trend their trend was compared to normalized patterns. The two normalized patterns describe an ideal quadratic trend are shown in figure 4.11. The pattern on the left describes a concave function, the one on the left a convex function.

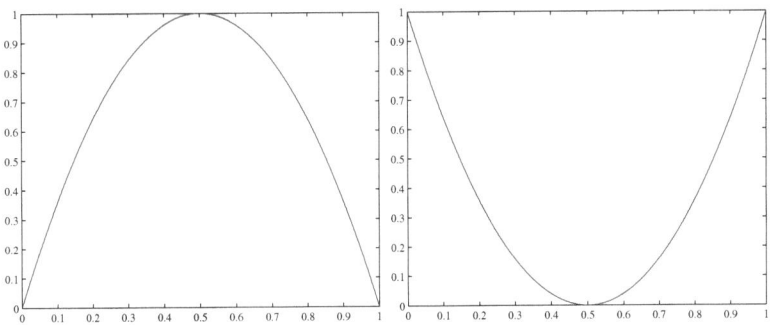

Figure 4.11: Normalized patterns to detect circadian trends.

To assess the circadian behavior of a variable the circadian model of each variable was normalized to a value range of 0 to 1. This normalized circadian trend is compared to the two patterns. The distance of the data points to the pattern is calculated by subtracting the values of the circadian model from the corresponding values of the circadian pattern. The result is a vector of differences, one for each time slice of the circadian model. The smaller the absolute values are, the more the circadian model follows the trend of the pattern.

The standard deviation of the absolute values of the vector of differences seems to be a suitable measure to describe the circadian behavior of a variable. The variables in the result section are therefore ranked by the standard deviation of the vector of differences.

We decided to use this evaluation procedure as it allows the comparison if all variables to a neutral reference curve. In earlier attempts we calculated the fit of the variables to quadratic regression curves but abandoned this approach because of its inability to compare the variables on a common basis.

4.5.3 Trends following the 3-Process Model

The model of daytime sleepiness and alertness based on Achermann and Borbély's 3-process model is explained in section 3.3. Besides the analysis of trends, which correspond with single processes of this model, the data is also analyzed to find variables that correspond with the actual model of sleepiness and alertness during daytime.

The model is based on a timescale, which corresponds to real date and time. Therefore the timescale of the data does not have to be altered. The same concept of aggregation of the data per time slice is applied. Time slices that correspond to 5 % of 24 hours were used, the same slice size as for the analysis of homeostatic trends.

The units of the amplitude of the 3-process model are 'arbitrary units'. As the focus is on trends of sleepiness and vigilance the model's internal numerical values were not mapped to more meaningful units. The EEG-based variables' value range was scaled to fit the model. The minimal value of the variable was mapped on the two recording days to the minimal value of the model on the corresponding two days. The analogous procedure was applied for the maxima.

An example of this mapping can be seen in figure 5.10. In the example the mapping of the subjective sleepiness rating on the KSS (red) to the model of sleepiness (blue) is shown.

To evaluate the goodness of fit of a variable to the model of either alertness or sleepiness a procedure similar to the analysis of circadian trends was applied. The distance of every data point to the value of the simulated curve was measured at the same point in time, resulting in a vector of differences. The standard deviation of the absolute values of the difference vectors was used to rank the suitability of the variables.

4.5.4 Separation of the two Conditions

The second hypothesis states that EEG-based variables exist that are able to distinguish the data from the days after the normal night and the recordings under sleep deprivation. The goal is to give empirical evidence that some of the variables fulfill this assumption.

A timescale relative to the time of waking up was chosen for this analysis. The raw data was described following the aggregation and normalization procedure described in section 4.5.1. The result is a model for each variable consisting of a daytime trend for sleep deprived sessions and a trend for the days after the normal nights. The values of these two trends are compared statistically to show that they differ significantly.

The pairs of values from the normal and sleep deprived sessions are analyzed using a paired t-test. The null hypothesis of this test assumes that the mean of the differences of the pairs is zero. The difference of the two trends is significant, if the null hypothesis can be rejected.

In the result section the variables are ranked by the mean difference of the pairs. The probability of the null hypothesis, which has to be lower than 5 % in order to have a significant result, is also shown.

4.5.5 Classification of Daytime Trends

In the preceding sections the analysis of aggregated data is described. The intention was to make a global statement about trends of EEG-based variables. This kind of analysis has a descriptive character and uncovers phenomena on a statistical level. In this section an application is described that goes a step further: the classification of daytime EEG data.

The intention is to find relevant variables, which make it possible to classify daytime EEG recordings, whether they were recorded under sleep deprivation or after a preceding night with normal sleep.

The classification algorithm is based on the model that uses the time of waking up as the temporal reference (section 4.5.1). The normalized data from the subjects is used to generate a trend for the days with sleep deprivation and one for the normal days. These trends are used as the reference trends for the two conditions.

Based on the reference trends the daytime EEG-recordings are classified. The aggregated and normalized trend for that session of a subject and the difference to the two reference trends for every time slice is calculated. The smaller of the two differences the classification of the time slice as sleep deprived or normal. This procedure is repeated for every slice and calculate a majority vote. If more slices were classified as sleep deprived than normal, the whole recording is classified as sleep deprived.

This voting procedure is visualized in figure 4.12. The bold curves in the two figures represent the reference model, the thin black line the session to be classified. The majority of data points on the left side is classified as a normal day, therefore the whole daytime trend is classified as normal. On the right side another example is shown. This time the votes for sleep-deprivation predominate, the session is classified as sleep deprived.

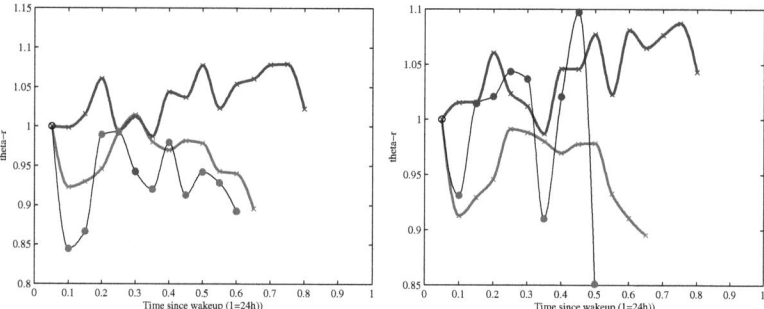

Figure 4.12: Classification of a session based on a reference model using distance voting. The red lines represent the model for the relative theta power after normal sleep, the blue line the model for the day under sleep deprivation. The black lines are classified according to the distance to the models. The left session is classified as normal session, the right one as sleep-deprived session.

Combination of variables In order to assess the performance of the combination of multiple variables the concept of classification is expanded. This was realized in a straight forward way: for any uneven number of variables a majority voting algorithm is implemented. The session is classified using each variable and then it is decided by majority vote how to ultimately classify the session.

4.5 Validation Strategies

Validation of classification performance   To assess the suitability of the EEG-based variables to correctly classify daytime recordings a procedure based on leave-one-out cross-validation (LOOCV) is used.

The concept of cross-validation is used, to assess how well statistical findings are applicable to independent datasets. In k-fold cross-validation the available n datasets are split up in k groups. The datasets from $k-1$ groups are used to build a model and the datasets from the remaining group are used for validation. This remaining group is also called the validation set, the other groups are called the training set. The performance can be measured by calculating an error between the results from the training set and the validation set. To get more accurate values of the performance this process is repeated by changing the training and test sets. This procedure is repeated k times, until every of the k groups of data sets was once used as validation set. The average of the errors calculated for every cycle is used as an over all measure of performance.

The LOOCV is a special case of cross-validation, where $n = k$. Every data set is its own group and used as validation set, resulting in n validation cycles.

The method of validation is based on LOOCV. The reference daytime trends are calculated for a variable using $n-1$ subjects and try to correctly classify the daytime trends of the remaining subject. The classification procedure described above is used and it is verified, if the classification was correct or wrong. We repeat this verification for every n subjects and calculate the fraction of correct classifications. The result is a fraction of correct classification for every EEG-based variable. The tables in the result section are ranked by this fraction.

χ^2 **independence test**   Additionally it is assessed, whether the classification is really working or could be caused by chance. For this purpose Pearson's χ^2 independence test is used.

A contingency table is built containing the number of correct and wrong results from the method and compare it to a choice by chance, which is assumed to be 50 % correct and 50 % wrong. The χ^2 independence test can tell, whether the difference in the correct classification rate of the two methods is significant or not. Pearson's χ^2 criterion is a measure, which expresses the difference between the two ways of classification.

The expected frequency for every cell of the table of 2x2 cells is calculated:
$$E_{i,j} = \frac{(O_{i,1} + O_{i,2}) * (O_{1,j} + O_{2,j})}{4},$$
with $O_{i,j}$ being the observed frequency in a cell. The resulting test statistic is
$$\chi^2 = \sum_{i=1}^{2} \sum_{j=1}^{2} \frac{O_{i,j} - E_{i,j}}{E_{i,j}}.$$
The null hypothesis can be rejected, if χ^2 is $\geq$ than the 95 % quantile of the χ^2-distribution with 1 degree of freedom.

Chapter 5

Results

In this chapter the results of the evaluation of the study data are presented. The employed procedures are described in section 4.5 and the evaluations are presented in the same order.

Many figures show the data in an aggregated form. As additional information the standard error (SE) of the aggregated values is shown, which is indicated as error bars or as dashed line below and above the aggregated values.

All EEG-based results presented here, are derived from the central recording positions C3-A2 and C4-A1, which were preprocessed according to section 4.2.

5.1 Subjects

26 subjects were recruited successfully, with 13 subjects in each of the two groups representing the cross-over design of the study. In group 1 the subjects had their recording session with normal sleep first and the night with sleep deprivation afterwards. In group 2 the two sessions were conducted the other way around.

The following table presents a basic statistical overview of the sample of subjects with an analysis of the subjects' age, their gender, and the PSQI. The values enlisted are mean values ± the SE. The values for gender are given proportionally.

	All (n=26)	Group 1 (n=13)	Group2 (n=13)
Age	28.077 ± 0.672	27.692 ± 0.990	28.462 ± 0.938
Gender (m/f)	0.58 / 0.42	0.62 / 0.38	0.54 / 0.46
PSQI	03.423 ± 0.209	03.615 ± 0.241	03.231 ± 0.343

The subjects recruited for the study were required to be healthy and good sleepers. That was ensured by the strict evaluation of the PSQI. The index had to lie below a value of 6. This fact is also reflected in the sleep-diary data, which the subjects collected for two weeks (figure A.6). The questionnaire is explained in detail in section 4.1.7.

The following table shows a statistical overview of the mean values of all subjects (n=26) ± the SE is presented. The same data is visualized in figure 5.1 by using boxplots. The statistical evaluation includes the data of all 26 recruited subjects. The arithmetic mean of all recorded values of each subject was calculated to generate this overview.

An example of the results of the sleep diary data for one subject is shown in figure 5.2.

	mean ± SE
Sleep Quality	09.661 ± 0.381
Wakeup Quality	13.117 ± 0.469
Physical Quality	05.503 ± 0.133
Summed Quality	28.247 ± 0.751

5.1.1 Data Quality

In the study design a drop-out rate of 23 % of the subjects was estimated. The following table shows the number of subjects with sufficient data quality in each category.

	All Subjects (n=26)	Group 1 (n=13)	Group 2 (n=13)
Biosignals night	26	13	13
Biosignals day	21	10	11
RTT	22	10	12
KSS	26	13	13
Actigraphy	23	11	12
SSA	26	13	13

5.1 Subjects

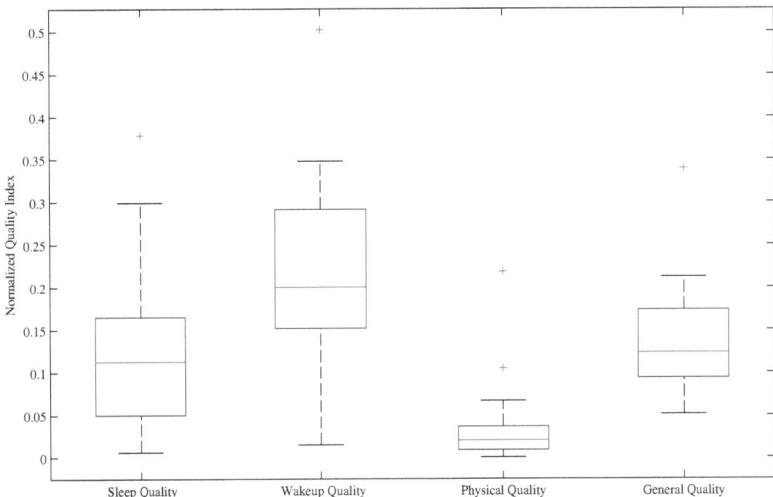

Figure 5.1: The boxplots visualize the aggregated values of the sleep-quality, wakeup-quality, physical condition, and a general quality measure for all 26 subjects included in the study. The boxes represent the median, the first, and the third quartile. The whisker show 1.5 times the interquartile range and the outliers are marked with the symbol '+'.

The reasons for insufficient data quality were mainly caused by technical problems and by subjects, who did not follow the study protocol. The reasons for insufficient data quality of the biosignals during daytime were broken batteries and electrodes that fell off. Some subjects did not handle the reaction time test application correctly, which led to unsaved and lost data. The actigraphy stopped working in some cases because of a defective actigraphy device.

All together it was possible to acquire 20 complete data sets from this study. This outcome perfectly fits the estimated drop-out ratio of 23 %.

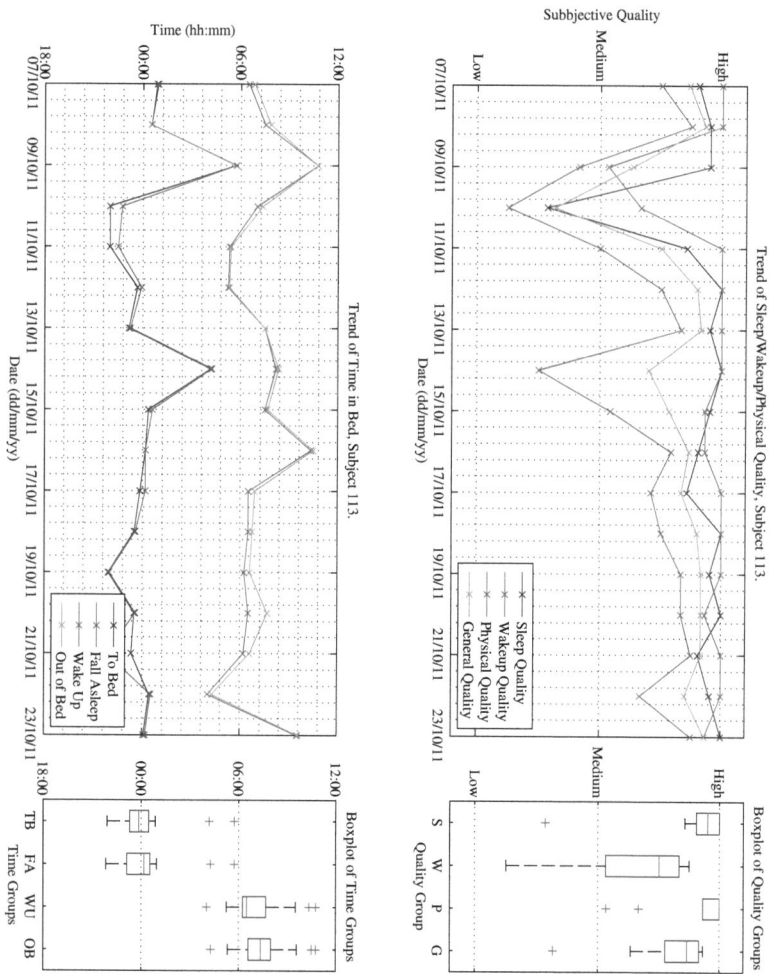

Figure 5.2: This figure shows the results of the sleep diary data of an exemplary subject. The upper part shows the trend of the quality measures over 2 weeks. The quality data was normalized to a qualitative scale. The sleep times are visualized in the lower part. The trends' data points are also visualized as boxplots on the right side of the figure.

5.2 Homeostatic Trends

Kendall's τ is used as a measure of linear correlation between the time since wake up and the normalized values of the variables. To find the variables that show the strongest homeostatic trend, all variables are ranked by their τ value. Additionally the significance of the τ value is indicated. If the null-hypothesis could be sufficiently rejected by a p value of smaller then 0.05, this is indicated with a star.

On the left side of table 5.1 the ranking of the best 10 variables for the 20 daytime sessions after normal sleep are enlisted, on the right side of table 5.1 the rankings for the mean τ values of the 20 sessions after sleep deprivation. For the normal sessions the relative beta power (theta-r) has the strongest trend, with a significant value of $\tau = 0.692$. The strongest correlation for the sessions after sleep deprivation is reached by the EOG artifacts (art-eog) with a significant value of $\tau = -0.765$.

The ranking of the mean τ of all 40 sessions independent of the recording condition is shown in table 5.2. The best performing variable for all sessions are the EOG artifacts (art-eog) with a very strong significant correlation of $\tau = -0.853$.

Additionally the most prominent linear trends are visualized. In figure 5.3 the strong negative correlation of EOG artifacts (art-eog) with the time after waking up is shown. The trends for the normal session and the sleep-deprived sessions do not differ. The strong positive homeostatic trend for the relative beta power (beta-r) is visualized in figure 5.4. The trend for the normal sessions is clearly stronger than for the sleep deprived sessions.

Variable	τ	Sig	Variable	τ	Sig
Normal sessions (n=20)			Sleep deprived sessions (n=20)		
beta-r	0.692	0.0005[*]	art-eog	-0.765	0.0000[*]
theta-alpha-beta	-0.692	0.0005[*]	alpha2	0.567	0.0017[*]
beta2	0.615	0.0027[*]	theta-r	0.550	0.0024[*]
art-eog	-0.604	0.0020[*]	alpha2-std	0.483	0.0086[*]
beta	0.564	0.0067[*]	pei	0.483	0.0086[*]
beta2-std	0.538	0.0101[*]	art-amplitude	0.477	0.0258[*]
beta3	0.538	0.0101[*]	art-no-variance	0.477	0.0258[*]
art-no-variance	0.524	0.0291[*]	beta-r	0.467	0.0115[*]
theta-event	-0.507	0.0218[*]	beta1	0.417	0.0255[*]
beta3-std	0.487	0.0216[*]	sef95	0.417	0.0255[*]
sef95	0.487	0.0216[*]	beta1-std	0.400	0.0326[*]
kurtosis	0.487	0.0216[*]	gamma-r	0.383	0.0413[*]
gamma1-std	0.462	0.0305[*]	alpha-factor	0.367	0.0517[ ]
beta-std	0.462	0.0305[*]	beta	0.367	0.0517[ ]
gamma1	0.462	0.0305[*]	alpha	0.367	0.0517[ ]
gamma-std	0.436	0.0422[*]	fail	0.351	0.1097[ ]
gamma	0.410	0.0573[ ]	alpha-event	0.343	0.0714[ ]
gamma2-std	0.385	0.0763[ ]	art-low-abs	0.343	0.1258[ ]
gamma-r	0.385	0.0763[ ]	alpha-std	0.333	0.0788[ ]

Table 5.1: Ranking of homeostatic trends after normal sleep and sleep deprivation.

5.2 Homeostatic Trends

Variable	Kendall τ	Significance
Correlation all sessions (n=40)		
art-eog	-0.853	0.0000[*]
alpha2	0.683	0.0001[*]
theta-r	0.667	0.0001[*]
alpha2-std	0.633	0.0003[*]
beta-r	0.533	0.0033[*]
alpha	0.483	0.0086[*]
art-amplitude	0.477	0.0258[*]
art-no-variance	0.477	0.0258[*]
theta-pause	-0.467	0.0115[*]
alpha-std	0.433	0.0198[*]
alpha1	0.433	0.0198[*]
beta1-std	0.417	0.0255[*]
beta1	0.417	0.0255[*]
alpha-factor	0.400	0.0326[*]
alpha-event	0.400	0.0326[*]
beta	0.400	0.0326[*]
delta-r	-0.383	0.0413[*]
pei	0.383	0.0413[*]
spindles	0.353	0.0518[ ]

Table 5.2: Ranking of the homeostatic trends of the model of all sessions.

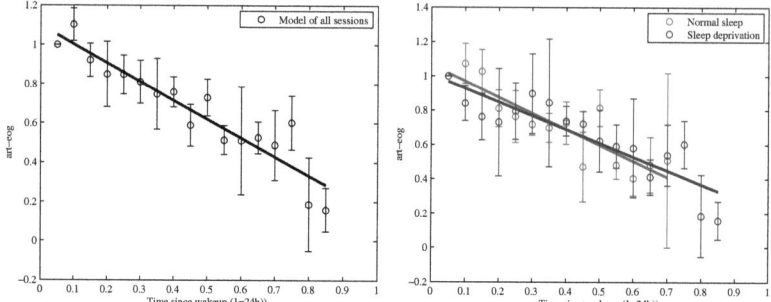

Figure 5.3: This figure shows the homeostatic trend of the model of EOG artifacts (art-eog). The data points of the model are shown as circles. The SE for each data point is shown as an error bar. A linear regression line is superimposed. The trend of all 40 sessions is shown on the left, the normal (red) and sleep deprived (blue) sessions are shown on the right.

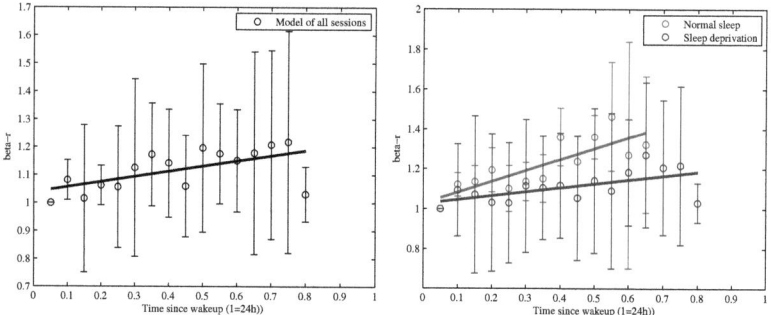

Figure 5.4: This figure shows the homeostatic trend of the model of the relative beta power (beta-r). The data points of the model are shown as circles. The SE for each data point is shown as an error bar. A linear regression line is superimposed. The trend of all 40 sessions is shown on the left, the normal (red) and sleep deprived (blue) sessions are shown on the right.

5.2 Homeostatic Trends

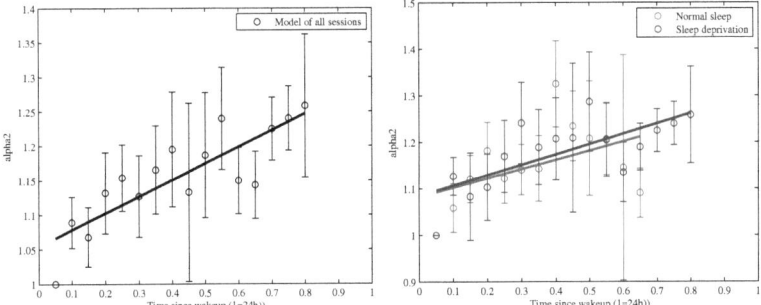

Figure 5.5: This figure shows the homeostatic trend of the model of the high alpha power (alpha2). The data points of the model are shown as circles. The SE for each data point is shown as an error bar. A linear regression line is superimposed. The trend of all 40 sessions is shown on the left, the normal (red) and sleep deprived (blue) sessions are shown on the right.

5.3 Circadian Trends

As described in section 4.5 the circadian trends of the models of each variable was evaluated. The models covering all 40 sessions were analyzed. To cover all session at once is valid because the two conditions, sufficient sleep and sleep deprivation, do not influence circadian trends.

The 20 variables with the strongest resemblance to the concave reference pattern are enlisted on the left side of table 5.3. The variables are ranked in ascending order by the standard deviation of the values of the vector of differences. The theta factor (theta-factor) is the feature with the strongest concave circadian behavior. The model of theta-factor is also shown in figure 5.6.

The 10 best performing variables regarding the convex reference pattern are enlisted in the right side of table 5.3. The variable with the strongest convex circadian behavior is not an EEG-based variable, but the subjective sleepiness ratings in the KSS, which is visualized in figure 5.8.

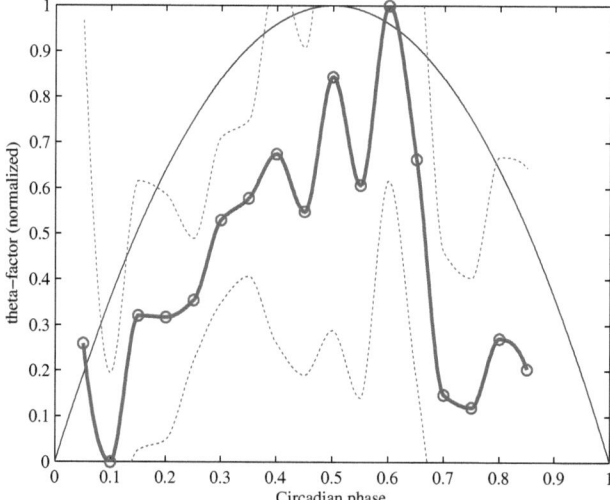

Figure 5.6: The theta factor (theta-factor) is visualized as an example for concave circadian behavior. The circles represent the aggregated values of all 40 sessions, the dashed lines show the SE.

5.3 Circadian Trends

Variable	STD of distance	Variable	STD of distance
Concave Pattern		Convex Pattern	
theta-factor	0.125	kss	0.120
theta	0.158	theta-pause	0.165
delta	0.165	art-general	0.180
alpha1	0.173	alpha-pause	0.186
alpha2	0.177	alpha-theta	0.188
alpha	0.181	theta-alpha-beta	0.192
beta1-std	0.181	sef95	0.194
theta-std	0.181	theta-r	0.200
beta1	0.182	pei	0.200
theta-event	0.183	art-no-variance	0.201
alpha2-std	0.184	art-amplitude	0.201
alpha-factor	0.186	kurtosis	0.204
alpha-std	0.187	delta-r	0.206
alpha1-std	0.190	gamma-std	0.207
beta3-std	0.192	gamma1-std	0.208
delta-std	0.192	alpha-r	0.208
beta2-std	0.194	alpha-event	0.209
art-high-rel	0.195	rem	0.210
beta-std	0.196	gamma2-std	0.211

Table 5.3: Ranking of variables' circadian trends following a concave and convex pattern.

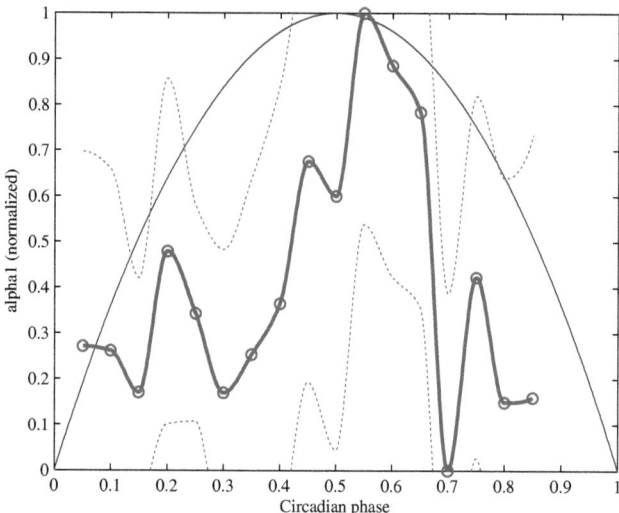

Figure 5.7: The concave circadian behavior of the low alpha activity (alpha1) is visualized in this figure. The circles represent the aggregated values of all 40 sessions, the dashed lines show the SE.

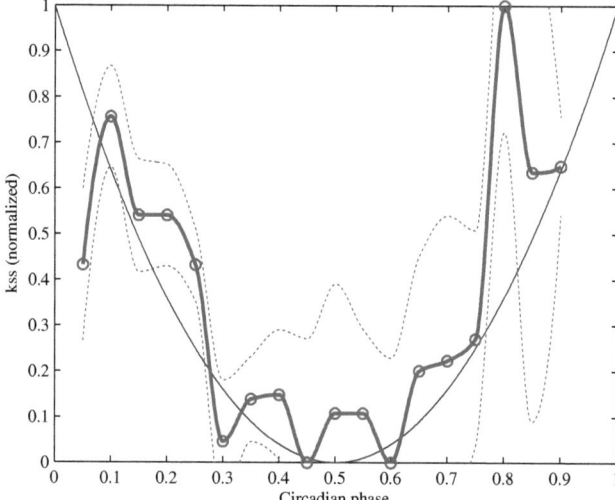

Figure 5.8: The convex circadian behavior of the (kss) is shown in this figure. The circles represent the aggregated values of all 40 sessions, the dashed lines show the SE.

5.3 Circadian Trends

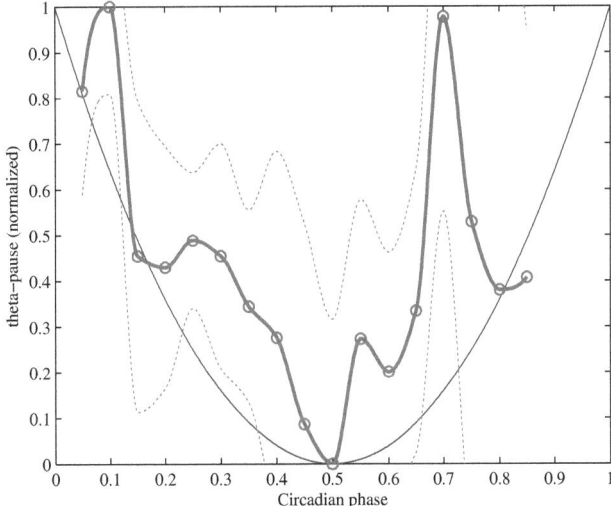

Figure 5.9: This figure shows the convex circadian behavior of the average duration of the pauses between theta events (theta-pause). The circles represent the aggregated values of all 40 sessions, the dashed lines show the SE.

5.4 Trends Following the 3-Process Model

In this section the results of the analysis of behavior according to the simulation of sleepiness and alertness following the 3-process model are presented. The standard deviation of the vector of differences between the variables and the simulation is used to rank the variables. The results for the simulation of alertness are presented on the left side of table 5.4. The 20 variables that have the most resemblance to the simulation of sleepiness are shown on the right side of table 5.4. The KSS ratings are the best performing parameter. The model of these ratings is superimposed on the mean simulation of sleepiness or all subjects in figure 5.10.

Variable	STD of distance	Variable	STD of distance
Simulation of Alertness		Simulation of Sleepiness	
theta-event	0.592	kss	0.444
beta1-std	0.606	theta-pause	0.525
rem	0.612	alpha-pause	0.532
beta-std	0.619	sem	0.582
alpha2-std	0.621	gamma-r	0.582
beta3-std	0.627	beta-r	0.591
beta2-std	0.629	delta-r	0.601
gamma-std	0.629	beta3	0.603
gamma1-std	0.632	rem	0.604
beta1	0.634	gamma2	0.608
alpha-event	0.634	theta-r	0.609
gamma2-std	0.637	gamma	0.611
theta-r	0.637	alpha-theta	0.612
delta-r	0.641	gamma1	0.613
pei	0.651	beta3-std	0.614
alpha2	0.651	gamma2-std	0.615
beta	0.654	gamma-std	0.615
beta3	0.654	art-general	0.616
sef95	0.656	art-eog	0.617
kurtosis	0.657	alpha-r	0.617

Table 5.4: Ranking of the variables following the simulation of alertness and sleepiness.

5.4 Trends Following the 3-Process Model 133

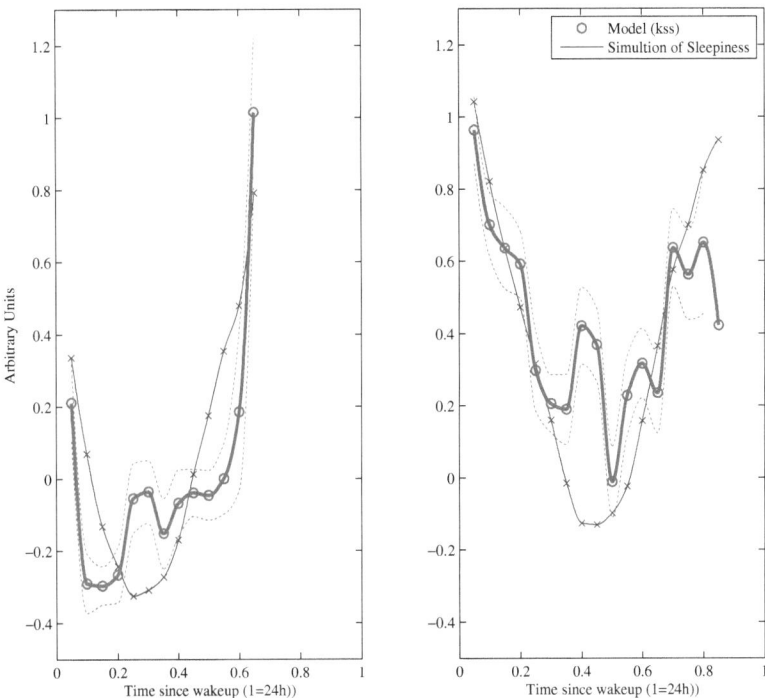

Figure 5.10: The figures show the mean simulation of sleepiness for all 20 subjects according to the 3-process model in blue color. The mean subjective sleepiness ratings on the KSS are superimposed in red color. The circles represent the aggregated data values, the dashed lines the SE. The left figure shows the day after normal sleep, the right figure visualizes the data on the day after sleep deprivation.

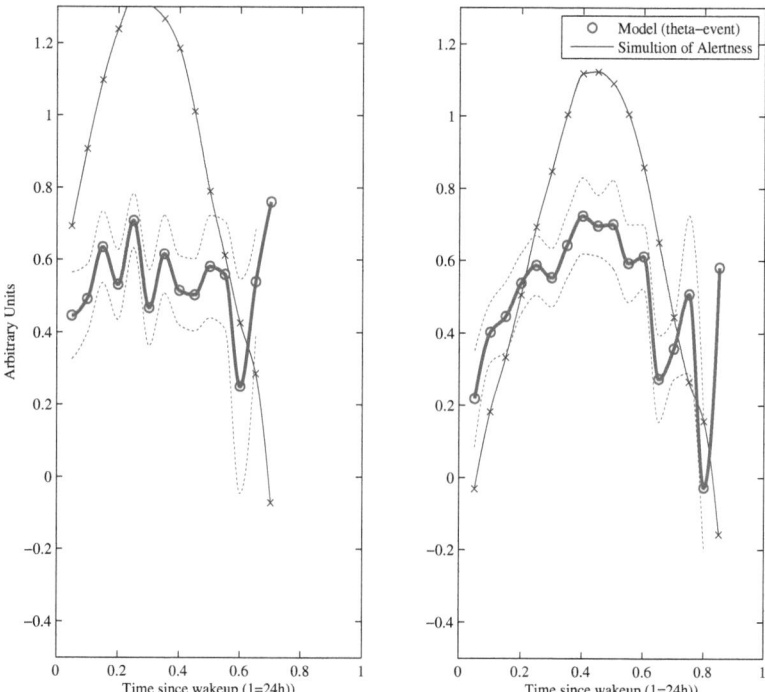

Figure 5.11: The figures show the mean simulation of alertness for all 20 subjects according to the 3-process model in blue color. The model of the mean duration of theta events (theta-event) is superimposed in red color. The circles represent the aggregated data values, the dashed lines the SE. The left figure shows the day after normal sleep, the right figure visualizes the data on the day after sleep deprivation.

5.5 Separability

In this section the results for variables are presented that provide proof for the second hypothesis, the ability to distinguish between different levels of vigilance, especially in normal and sleep-deprived sessions. The variables are ranked according to their statistical values of the paired t-test. The 10 best performing variables are shown in table 5.5.

The (theta-factor) is the best separating variable with an average mean difference of all time slices with a value of -6.438. The second best variable is the relative theta power (theta-r), which is visualized in figure 5.12.

Variable	Paired t-test	Significance
theta-factor	-6.824	0.0000[*]
theta-event	-5.811	0.0001[*]
theta-r	-5.240	0.0002[*]
theta-std	-5.184	0.0002[*]
theta	-5.147	0.0002[*]
art-high-rel	-4.428	0.0007[*]
theta-pause	4.395	0.0009[*]
theta-alpha-beta	-3.934	0.0020[*]
beta-r	3.928	0.0020[*]
delta-r	3.650	0.0033[*]
sef95	2.841	0.0149[*]
alpha-r	-2.728	0.0183[*]
spindles	-2.603	0.0219[*]
gamma-r	2.530	0.0264[*]
beta3	2.416	0.0326[*]
react	2.411	0.0329[*]
gamma1-std	2.375	0.0351[*]
beta	2.339	0.0375[*]
kurtosis	2.265	0.0428[*]
gamma2-std	2.251	0.0440[*]
beta3-std	2.154	0.0523[ ]

Table 5.5: Ranking of the performance of the variables in separating the two conditions.

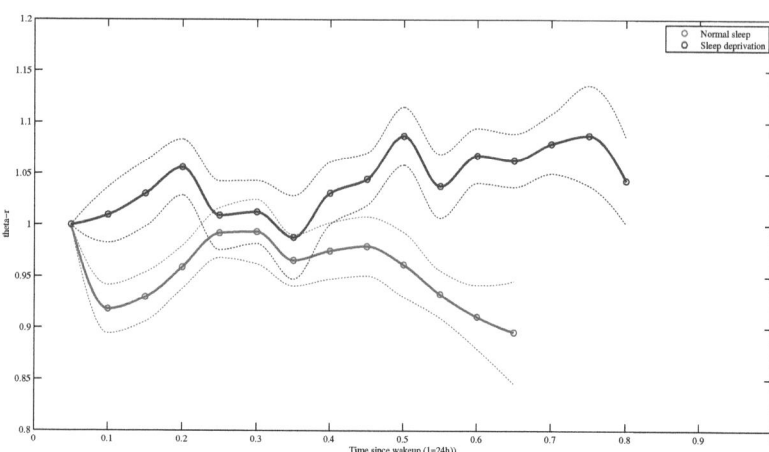

Figure 5.12: This figure shows the model of the 20 normal and 20 sessions under sleep deprivation based on the relative theta power (theta-r). The SE of the values is visualized as the dashed line. The feature can be used to separate the two kinds of sessions.

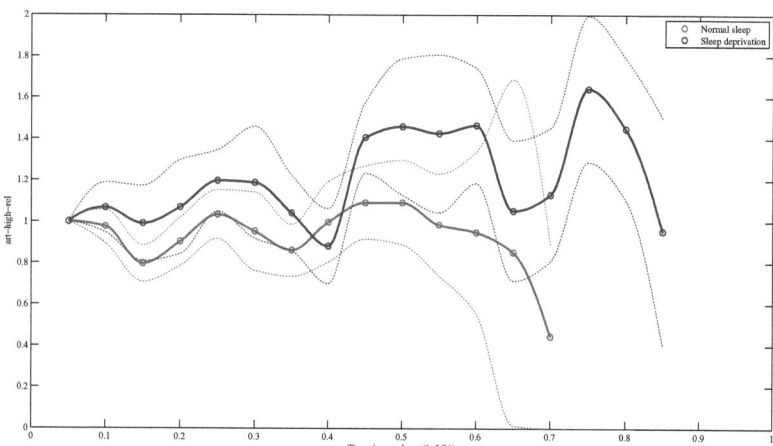

Figure 5.13: This example shows the model of the artifacts, where the relative frequency is too high (art-high-rel). This variable is perfectly suitable to separate sleep deprived from normal sessions.

5.5 Separability

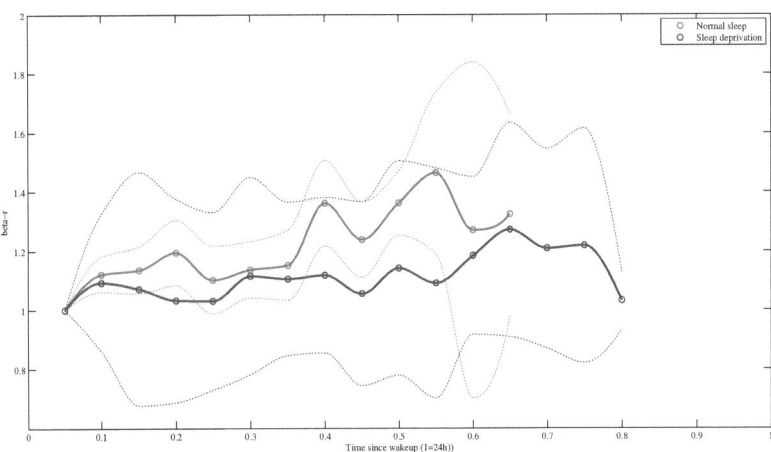

Figure 5.14: This example shows the model of the relative beta power (beta-r). It can significantly separate between the normal and sleep deprived condition.

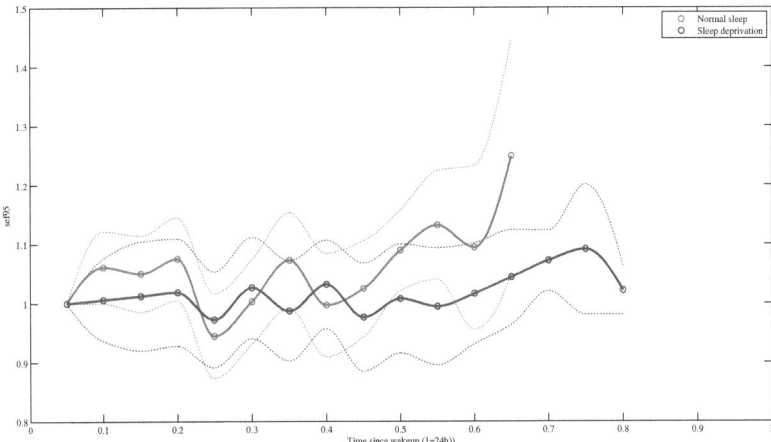

Figure 5.15: This second example shows the model of the spectral edge frequency at 95% (sef95). The SEF95 variable is significantly able to separate normal from sleep deprived sessions.

5.6 Model-based Classification

As described in section 4.5 the χ^2 test was chosen to evaluate the performance of the variables in classifying sessions. In this section the rankings of variable performance are presented. The 10 variables best classifying normal sessions are enlisted in table 5.6. The EOG artifacts (art-eog)are the best performing parameter, with a mean correctness of 70 %. According to the χ^2 test the result is not significantly. Table 5.7 enlists the ranking of variables' performance in classifying sleep-deprived sessions. The standard deviation of the very high beta band (beta3-std) is the best variable with a mean performance of 80 % correctness. This result is significant according to the χ^2 test.

In table 5.8 the ranking of variables is shown according to their general classification performance of all 40 sessions. The best performing parameter is again the very high beta standard deviation with a mean correctness of 70 %. This result is not significant. It was explained earlier that the performance of combination of variables for classifying daytime EEG-recordings was analyzed. The 10 best performing variables from table 5.8 were chosen and all 120 combinations of three variables were tested. Table 5.9 shows the 10 best performing combinations of variables in classifying sessions. 33 of the 120 possible combination show a significant results with levels of correctness between 80 % and 72.5 %.

Variable	Correct Classification	χ^2 Significance	Sessions
art-eog	0.700 ± 0.105	0.1967[ ]	20
theta-factor	0.700 ± 0.105	0.1967[ ]	20
delta-r	0.700 ± 0.105	0.1967[ ]	20
beta2	0.700 ± 0.105	0.1967[ ]	20
art-general	0.650 ± 0.109	0.3373[ ]	20
theta-std	0.650 ± 0.109	0.3373[ ]	20
theta-r	0.650 ± 0.109	0.3373[ ]	20
theta-alpha-beta	0.650 ± 0.109	0.3373[ ]	20
theta-pause	0.600 ± 0.112	0.5250[ ]	20
beta3-std	0.600 ± 0.112	0.5250[ ]	20

Table 5.6: Ranking of the variables' performance in classifying normal sessions.

5.6 Model-based Classification

Variable	Correct Classification	χ^2 Significance	Sessions
beta3-std	0.800 ± 0.092	0.0467[*]	20
gamma1-std	0.750 ± 0.099	0.1025[ ]	20
art-high-abs	0.700 ± 0.105	0.1967[ ]	20
gamma1	0.700 ± 0.105	0.1967[ ]	20
beta3	0.700 ± 0.105	0.1967[ ]	20
sem	0.650 ± 0.109	0.3373[ ]	20
theta-factor	0.650 ± 0.109	0.3373[ ]	20
theta-pause	0.650 ± 0.109	0.3373[ ]	20
theta-event	0.650 ± 0.109	0.3373[ ]	20
gamma2-std	0.650 ± 0.109	0.3373[ ]	20

Table 5.7: Ranking of the variables' performance in classifying sleep deprived sessions.

Variable	Correct Classification	χ^2 Significance	Sessions
beta3-std	0.700 ± 0.073	0.0679[ ]	40
theta-factor	0.675 ± 0.075	0.1119[ ]	40
theta-std	0.650 ± 0.076	0.1748[ ]	40
theta-r	0.650 ± 0.076	0.1748[ ]	40
delta-r	0.650 ± 0.076	0.1748[ ]	40
art-high-abs	0.625 ± 0.078	0.2598[ ]	40
art-general	0.625 ± 0.078	0.2598[ ]	40
gamma1-std	0.625 ± 0.078	0.2598[ ]	40
theta-alpha-beta	0.625 ± 0.078	0.2598[ ]	40
art-eog	0.600 ± 0.078	0.3687[ ]	40

Table 5.8: Ranking of the variables' performance in classifying all sessions.

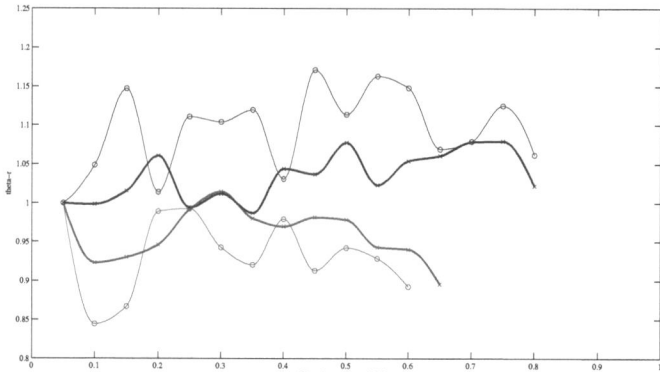

Figure 5.16: This figure shows a classification example based on the relative theta power (theta-r). The model for normal (red) and sleep deprived (blue) sessions is visualized with the bold lines. Two sessions of the same subject (thin lines) are correctly classified by the models.

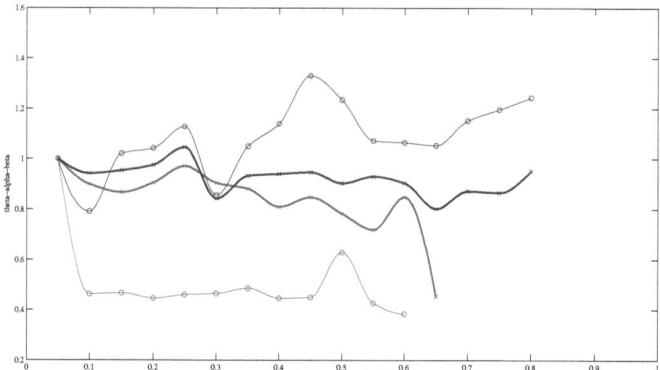

Figure 5.17: This figure shows a classification example based on the $(\theta + \alpha)/\beta$ ratio (theta-alpha-beta). The model is able to classify the two exemplary sessions (the thin lines) correctly.

5.6 Model-based Classification

Combination of 3 Variables			Correct Classification	χ^2 Sig	n
beta3-std	theta-factor	art-eog	0.8000	0.0049[*]	40
beta3-std	theta-std	art-eog	0.8000	0.0049[*]	40
beta3-std	delta-r	art-high-abs	0.8000	0.0049[*]	40
beta3-std	theta-factor	art-general	0.7750	0.0105[*]	40
beta3-std	theta-factor	art-high-abs	0.7750	0.0105[*]	40
beta3-std	theta-std	art-general	0.7750	0.0105[*]	40
beta3-std	delta-r	art-eog	0.7750	0.0105[*]	40
theta-r	delta-r	art-general	0.7750	0.0105[*]	40
delta-r	gamma1-std	art-high-abs	0.7750	0.0105[*]	40
beta3-std	theta-std	art-high-abs	0.7500	0.0209[*]	40
beta3-std	theta-r	art-eog	0.7500	0.0209[*]	40
beta3-std	delta-r	art-general	0.7500	0.0209[*]	40
beta3-std	art-high-abs	theta-alpha-beta	0.7500	0.0209[*]	40
theta-factor	theta-r	art-eog	0.7500	0.0209[*]	40
theta-factor	art-high-abs	art-eog	0.7500	0.0209[*]	40
theta-std	theta-r	art-eog	0.7500	0.0209[*]	40
beta3-std	theta-r	delta-r	0.7250	0.0389[*]	40
beta3-std	delta-r	theta-alpha-beta	0.7250	0.0389[*]	40
beta3-std	art-general	theta-alpha-beta	0.7250	0.0389[*]	40
theta-factor	delta-r	art-high-abs	0.7250	0.0389[*]	40

Table 5.9: This table shows the best performing combinations of variables in correctly classifying sessions.

Chapter 6

Discussion

The aim of this thesis was to provide EEG-based variables that can objectively quantify daytime trends vigilance. It was possible to confirm the two hypotheses defined in the introduction of chapter 4. Additionally the concept of describing trends was extended to the EEG-based classification of data.

In this chapter the validation of the hypothesis stating that EEG-based show daytime trends is discussed. The temporal aspects of the hypothesis are analyzed, providing evidence for the correlation of EEG-variables with the time awake. Such trends are called 'homeostatic' following the nomenclature of Achermann and Borbely [3]. Another temporal aspect is the correlation with the individual circadian phase. The third external relationship of variables which was analyzed is the correlation with the model of alertness and sleepiness according to the three-process model.

The second hypothesis could be confirmed, which states that the separation of the different vigilance levels - normal sleep and sleep deprivation - is possible based on the variables derived from brain activity.

All of our empirical results are based on the data acquired in the study. The exploratory character of the study and the number of complete data sets ($n = 20$) can lead to type 1 errors, which are false positive results and findings.

6.1 Homeostatic Trends

The time since wakeup corresponds to the homeostatic process in the 3-process model of Achermann and Borbély during daytime. It is also called 'sleep debt' in literature. The rankings of the best 20 variables can be found in tables 5.1 and 5.2.

The variable that is best correlated with this kind of behavior is the trend of EOG artifacts (art-eog) with a Kendall $\tau = -0.853$ for all 40 sessions. For the 20 normal sessions the EOG artifacts are the fourth best variable with $\tau = -0.604$ and for the sessions under sleep deprivation a value of $\tau = -0.765$ is reached, which is the best variable in this ranking. All other types of artifacts have an increasing daytime trend. The artifacts with a too high amplitude and EEG sections without variance increase moderately with a significant correlation coefficient of $\tau = 0.477$. The other types increase, but not significantly. The correlation coefficient of the overall artifact variable (art-general) is slightly and not significantly negative, which is mainly caused by the strong negative correlation of the EOG artifacts.

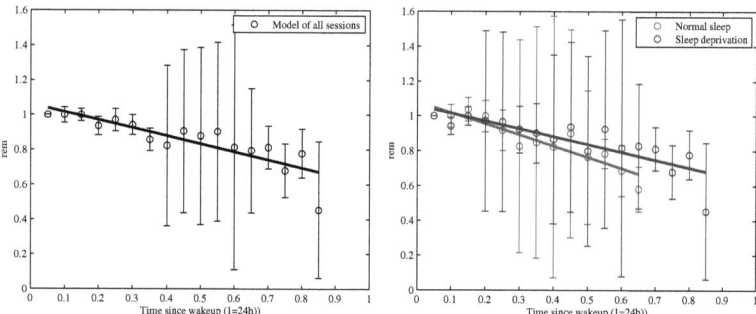

Figure 6.1: The homeostatic property of rapid eye movements derived from the EOG.

This strong decrease of EOG artifacts with the time awake has not yet been documented in literature. The physiological reasons for this phenomenon were further investigated by directly analyzing the EOG. Two variables were derived from the EOG for slow and rapid eye movements. The Somnolyzer 24x7 algorithm was used to classify slow and rapid eye movements in the EOG according to the AASM polysomnography guidelines. Following the procedure described for the spindles variable a variable for REM and SEM activity was calculated and the trend of the variables was analyzed over the day. The analysis clearly shows that the trend of EOG-artifacts is nearly identical with the

6.1 Homeostatic Trends

trend of REM activity. The REM variable shows a significant trend for normal sessions ($\tau = -0.7975$), sleep-deprived sessions ($\tau = -0.7749$), and all sessions with a τ value of -0.8253. The trends of SEMs are not significant and show a marginally decreasing trend for normal sessions ($\tau = -0.1922$), a slightly rising trend for sleep-deprived sessions ($\tau = 0.2844$) and an inconclusive trend for all sessions with $\tau = 0.1009$. Based on this result the EOG artifacts are nearly exclusively caused by REM activity in the EOG. Physiologically a decrease of the fraction of rapid eye movements with the time awake is responsible for this trend. The REM and SEM trends are visualized in figures 6.1 and 6.2.

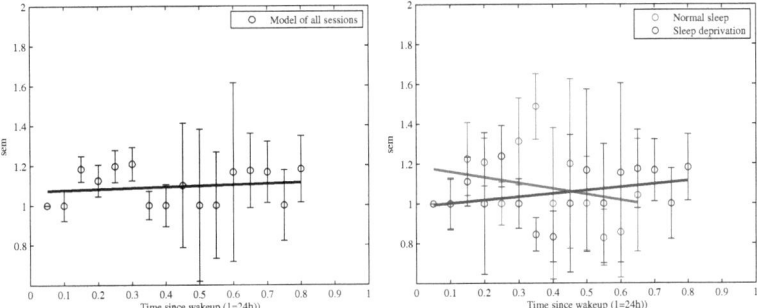

Figure 6.2: The homeostatic property of slow eye movements derived from the EOG.

The high alpha band (alpha2) from 11 Hz to 13.9 Hz shows the second best positive correlation of $\tau = 0.683$. The alpha band is usually referred to as a variable influenced by the circadian rhythm. Nevertheless a homeostatic behavior was discovered in its upper half-band.

Cajochen et al. [33] as well as Aeschbach et al. [5] describe an increase of theta and very low alpha activity from 6.3 Hz to 9 Hz during prolonged wakefulness. Their band does not overlap with our finding. The standard deviation of the band-filtered signal in the same band (alpha2-std) shows a similar behavior as the high alpha power ($\tau = 0.633$). The increase in the standard deviation of the higher alpha band could be explained by the event-like nature of alpha activity. An increase of such high-alpha events increases the standard deviation. The mean event length of the whole alpha band (alpha-event) also increases with a significant value of $\tau = 0.400$. This is additional evidence for the presence of the trend and supports the finding of an increase of the standard deviation of the alpha band.

The third best correlation with the time since waking up is present for the relative power in the theta frequency band (theta-r). This relative frequency band increases significantly with a strong correlation of $\tau = 0.667$. The correlation is not significant for the normal sessions and significantly moderate ($\tau = 0.550$) for the sleep-deprived sessions only. The findings correspond with results from other authors. Finelli et al. [54] present increasing theta power with an extended wakefulness of subjects over 40 hours. They recorded the EEG signals under a laboratory condition and non-continuously, but in recording sessions every 3 hours. Their results can be confirmed and also apply for the continuous real-world data.

The fifth strongest homeostatic trend for all 40 recorded sessions is the relative beta frequency power (beta-r), with a significant moderate $\tau = 0.588$. The relative beta power is the strongest correlating variable for the normal sessions with a significant value of $\tau = 0.736$ and is also significant for the sleep deprived sessions with a value of $\tau = 0.515$. The homeostatic modulation in the beta band confirms findings from extended wakefulness studies. Aeschbach et al. [5] conducted a laboratory study with prologued wakefulness of about 40 hours. The EEG was measure every 30 minutes. The positive beta trend can be confirmed and is also valid under real-world conditions. The increase in beta activity could be caused by the additional cognitive effort which is necessary to maintain the normal level of alertness with an increasing time of wakefulness.

6.2 Circadian trends

As explained earlier the circadian trends in the variables were analyzed according to a concave and a convex pattern. These two patterns describe the same phenomenon, but take the nature of a variable into account. The ones following the concave pattern have their minimum at the estimated minimum of the circadian rhythm, rise to a maximum after half the circadian period and fall again to minimum.

The variables which most prominently follow this trend are based on the theta frequency band and the alpha frequency band. The best matching variable is the theta-factor, which is explained in section 4.3.4 and visualized in figure 5.6. The theta-factor is followed by the absolute theta power in the ranking. The findings are supported by other authors, for instance Aeschbach et al. [6]. These author's findings are based on a 40 hour protocol with recordings in a laboratory environment in discrete 3 minute recordings every half hour. Aeschbach et al. describe the minimum of the theta activity cycle as 1 hour after the start of melatonin discretion. The minimum of the actigraphy-based circadian rhythm lies in average in the middle of the sleep time. The described circadian rhythm for theta activity has an offset of about +2 to +3 hours to the findings of Aeschbach et al.

The second prominent finding concerning concave circadian rhythms is the trend in the alpha bands. The absolute alpha power of the alpha band shows a circadian behavior, where the lower alpha-half-band has slightly more resemblance to the reference curve than the higher half-band. These findings are partly backed by the findings of Aeschbach et al. [6]. They describe a circadian rhythm in the higher alpha sub-band, where the minimum corresponds to the minimum in body temperature. The circadian rhythm of the body temperature has a phase offset similar to the actigraphy-based estimation [34].

Variables following the convex pattern behave inversely to the pattern described above. They have their maximum at the minimum of the actigraphy-based estimate of the circadian rhythm. The variable with the strongest convex circadian trend was not an EEG-based, but the subjective sleepiness ratings on the KSS. This finding confirms findings like the one from Cajochen et al. [34]. The authors of this publication clearly state that ratings on the KSS have a very strong circadian influence.

The general artifact variable (`art-general`) also show a trend resembling the convex reference function. No publication covering the circadian aspects of artifacts in continuous daytime EEG recordings could be found. The artifact variable shows a high variability, but nevertheless reaches a minimum around noon.

6.3 Model of Alertness and Sleepiness

In the previous two sections the homeostatic and circadian behavior of variables were discussed, which are the basic processes of Achermann and Borbély's 3-process model. The next step is the analysis of the performance of the variables when directly compared to the model of sleepiness and alertness, which is mainly based on the combination homeostatic and circadian process.

The subjective sleepiness rating on the KSS is the only variable that fits the model of sleepiness well. This behavior is known from literature and is documented e.g by Cajochen et al. [34]. The good performance of the KSS can be seen in figure 5.10. The KSS data from the normal sessions as well the data from the sleep deprived nicely follows the mean sleepiness model of all subjects.

For the other variables no comparable trends could be found. Some variables resemble the trend of the model under one condition but not for the other, for instance the variable theta-events is shown in figure 5.11. For the condition after normal sleep on the left side the variable does not at all fit the model. In contrast the variable resembles the model for alertness during the sleep deprivation. The same effect can be seen for the model of sleepiness, for instance for the theta-pause variable or the alpha-pause variable, which follows the trend of the model of sleepiness on the day with sleep deprivation. The trend on the day under the normal sleep condition does not correspond to the model.

6.4 Separability

The second hypothesis presented in the introduction states that it is possible to find variables that are able to separate data recorded under the normal sleep condition and data under sleep deprivation.

Following the procedure explained in section 4.5 a large number of variables was identified that are significantly able to separate the data from the two conditions.

The best performing variables are all based on the theta frequency band, they are the theta-factor, the relative theta power (theta-r), and the absolute theta power (theta). As an example the relative theta power is shown in figure 5.12.

According to the model of sleep homeostasis a sleep debt builds up during wakefulness, which is compensated by sleep. Insufficient sleep leads to an incomplete compensation of the sleep debt, which increases the base level of sleep debt on the subject's following day. All of the models are normalized relative to the first time slice of each session. If the increase of the sleep debt was a completely linear process, the models of the two conditions would not differ due to the normalization and the identical ascent. This is not the case. The model for the sleep-deprived condition rises clearly more steeply than the normal condition. This finding points at an exponential behavior of the theta variables, when they are used as an indicator for the sleep dept. This supports the conclusion from the analysis of homeostatic trends. The theta power is a variable validly representing the exponential behavior of the homeostatic process during wakefulness.

The second best performing variable after the theta-based variables are the relative-high-frequency-artifacts (`art-high-rel`). There is no evidence of a similar phenomenon in literature. The paired t-test clearly shows that the variable significantly differs for the two conditions. The trend of the model for sleep deprivation shows more artifacts of this kind, than for the normal sessions. Figure 5.13 also visually shows the clear separation between the two conditions based on this variable.

The spectral edge frequency at 95 % is shown in figure 5.15. According to the analysis, this variable is also suitable to separate the normal from the sleep deprived sessions. The SEF95 variable is higher for the normal sessions and has significantly lower values for the sleep deprived model. This result corresponds with the general understanding of the relation of levels of vigilance with the spectral components of the EEG. The higher the fraction of low frequency components, the lower is the value of the SEF95. As the frequency content of the EEG slows down generally during sleepiness and sleep deprivation the SEF95 has to be lower for the sleep deprived condition. Significant empirical evidence can be provided for this assumption.

6.5 Model-based Classification

An important result of this thesis are the results of the classification algorithm. Based on a literature review this is the first attempt to describe a model-based classification algorithm for daytime vigilance trends. Based on the procedure described in the method's section the variables' suitability to classify normal sessions, sleep-deprived sessions, and their all-over performance was evaluated.

For the normal sessions the best results were a mean correct classification of 70 %, as shown in table 5.6. This rate was reached for the EOG artifacts (`art-eog`), the `theta-factor`, the relative delta power (`delta-r`), and the absolute power of the mid-beta range (`beta2`). No result was significant according to the χ^2 test. The non-significance is caused by the low number of available sessions (n=20).

For the sleep-deprived sessions the results were better. They are shown in table 5.7. The best performing variable is the standard deviation of the high beta band (beta3-std) with a significant correctness of 80 %. The next best results with 75 % correctness is achieved by the standard deviation of the lowest gamma band (gamma1-std). This result is not significant.

The best result for all two types of sessions is the standard deviation for the highest beta band (bets3-std) with non-significant 70 % correct classification. None of the described parameters reaches a sufficient level of classification performance to serve as a classification model (table 5.8).

The ranking of the variables in table 5.8 was used as a preselection for the combination of parameters. All combinations of 3 variables for the 10 best performing variables were tested. 34 of the 120 possible combinations of three variables lead to a significant and good classification performance. The result is shown in table 5.9. Three combinations of variables reach a significant level of a classification correctness of 80 %. The variables are all based on the standard deviation of the very high beta band (beta3-std), the theta-factor, the standard deviation of the theta band (theta-std, the relative delta power (delta-r, the EOG artifacts (art-eog), and the muscle artifacts (art-high-abs).

It is shown the first time that EEG-variables based on delta-, theta-, and beta-frequency bands in combination with the trends of muscle and EOG artifacts are able to classify long-term EEG recordings correctly with a high probability. The chosen variables are sufficient to discriminate with a high probability between a day after normal sleep and a day after a night with insufficient sleep quality, in the 50 % of the normal sleep time.

The literature review shows that authors with the intention to classify stages of vigilance mostly rely on sophisticated classification algorithms, such as artificial neuronal networks, or Gaussian Mixture Models (see section 3.4.3.1.3). A major drawback of these methods is that the criteria of discrimination are not disclosed by the algorithm. The classification remains an algorithmic black-box. This also increases the risk of over fitting, which limits the results to exactly the data used for the development and tests of the algorithms.

The approach to classify EEG-based daytime trends was not driven by the goal to perfectly classify EEG data but an attempt to gain knowledge, which EEG-based variables show a suitable behavior. By combining EEG-based variables of different qualities (frequency-based and artifact-based) it was shown the first time that it is possible to classify EEG data correctly with a high profitability based on a very simple and straight forward classification system.

6.6 Future Research

6.6.1 Multi Modal Approach

The focus of this thesis was limited to the analysis of EEG-based variables. This limitation was chosen to specifically evaluate at which extent an EEG-only solution to the problem will succeed. Nevertheless it was clear from the beginning on that a multi-modal approach based on different biosignals could lead to a more robust model and clearer results. This assumption is based on evidence of multi-modal models in literature and the own experience. One example is the behavior of EOG artifacts as discussed in the section about homeostatic trends. The phenomenon in the EEG data already points at the strong relationship between the two biosignals. One of the next steps in this project will be a combination with variables from different biosignals, especially the EOG. The thesis was partly funded by the KlaVig project. This project has exactly this focus - the combination of EEG and EOG signals to build a robust model to objectively quantify vigilance based on physiological signals.

6.6.2 Additional Variables

The currently data analysis is based on the two central EEG channels only. The frontal and occipital channels were not yet analyzed nor were the channels compared to each other. There is evidence in literature that the synchrony between EEG channels may be a good indicator for the quantification of sleepiness and vigilance. There are also transient phenomena that can only be captured by using the regional information of the EEG channels. An example is the anteriorization of the alpha activity in the EEG during the onset of sleep.

6.6.3 Improve Classification

A very basic classification algorithm based on the EEG-derived variables was implemented in the course of this thesis. It was already mentioned that the focus of the thesis was the discovery of trends in EEG-based variables, not the perfect classification of EEG data. Nevertheless it is possible to build much more sophisticated classification models. Such a model could profit of the results of this thesis. The identified variables can serve as input-variables for such a classification algorithm. Such a classification algorithm could be based on technologies like artificial neuronal networks, Gaussian mixture models, or hidden Markov models.

6.6.4 Additional Evaluation

In the study a large number of different variables was recorded, for instance biosignals during the night, reaction times, subjective sleepiness ratings, and subjective sleep quality ratings. In the evaluation presented in this thesis the focus was on the behavior of variables with different time scales and were not able to cover all possible aspects.

The relationship of the EEG-based variables to the reaction times are a possible candidate for further analysis. Such an analysis could be very helpful in finding optimal variables to objectively quantify sleepiness in real-world situation were reaction times are known to be crucial.

All recorded 24-hour sessions consist of a night and a day. In this thesis the evaluation of the nights and their relationship to the following day was not covered. The data holds the potential to provide empirical evidence of the relationship between sleep quality variables to the vigilance trend of the following day.

Appendix A

Study Documents

In this appendix several documents from our study are presented.

In compliance with the guidelines for Scientific Good Practice of the Medical University of Vienna we applied for a vote of the Ethics Committee. The positive vote is shown in figures A.1 and A.2.

During the recruitment of the subjects participating in the study were informed thoroughly about the study protocol, possible risks, and the subject's rights and duties during the study. The informed consent document is shown in figures A.3 and A.4.

The subjects included in our study were required to be good sleepers. Their sleep quality was assessed based on the Pittsburgh Sleep Quality Index. The form is shown in the original german version in figure A.5.

As a part of the study protocol the subjects were monitored for two weeks. The subjects were instructed to complete a sleep- and wakeup-quality self-assessment form every morning. It is shown in figure A.6.

**ETHIK-KOMMISSION
DER MEDIZINISCHEN UNIVERSITÄT WIEN**
Borschkegasse 8b/6 - A-1090 Wien, Austria
☎ 0043 1 404 00 – 2147, 2244 & 📠 0043 1 404 00 – 1690
E-Mail: ethik-kom@meduniwien.ac.at
ethikkommission.meduniwien.ac.at

Sitzung der Ethik-Kommission am 05. Juli 2011, TOP 106 :

EK Nr: 622/2011
Antragsteller: Univ.Prof.DDr. Josef Zeitlhofer, Dipl. Ing. Gregor König
Einreichende Institution: Univ.Klin.f. Neurologie
Projekttitel: Eine explorative prospektive Studie zur Untersuchung von Wachsamkeit anhand EEG.

Die Stellungnahme der Ethik-Kommission erfolgt aufgrund folgender eingereichter Unterlagen:

Dokument	Version/Nr	Datiert
Originalprotokoll:	1.0/1.1	2011-05-30/2011-07-11
Probandeninfo./Einverständniserklrg.:	1.0/1.1	2011-05-30/2011-07-11
Verpflichtungserklärung:		undatiert
Qualifikation: CV, Conflict of Interest-Erklärung		undatiert

Die Kommission fasst folgenden Beschluss (mit X markiert):

☒ Es besteht kein Einwand gegen die Durchführung der Studie.

☐ Die unten bezeichneten Punkte des Antrages sind entweder noch unerledigt bzw sollten von den Antragstellern geändert/ nachgereicht werden. Nach entsprechender Vorlage/Erledigung kann auch vor der nächsten Ethik-Kommissions Sitzung ein endgültig positiver Beschluss ausgefertigt werden. Der Antrag wird in der nächsten Sitzung der Kommission nicht mehr behandelt.
<u>Achtung</u>: Werden die geforderten Unterlagen von den Antragstellern nicht innerhalb von 3 Sitzungsperioden (ab Datum dieser Sitzung) nachgereicht, gilt der Antrag ohne weitere Benachrichtigung als zurückgezogen und muss gegebenenfalls als Neuantrag eingereicht werden.

☐ Es bestehen Einwände gegen die Durchführung der Studie in der eingereichten Form. Die unten angeführten Punkte sollten von den Antragstellern entsprechend geändert und der Kommission neu vorgelegt werden. Der Antrag wird in der nächsten Sitzung der Kommission nochmals behandelt.
<u>Achtung</u>: Werden die geforderten Unterlagen von den Antragstellern nicht innerhalb von 3 Sitzungsperioden (ab Datum dieser Sitzung) nachgereicht, gilt der Antrag ohne weitere Benachrichtigung als zurückgezogen und muß gegebenenfalls als Neuantrag eingereicht werden.

☐ Der Antrag wird von der Ethik-Kommission abgelehnt.

☐ Der TOP wird bis zur nächsten Sitzung vertagt (Begründung siehe unten)

Figure A.1: The final vote of the ethics committee of the Medical University of Vienna, which agrees with the conduction of our study.

Kommentare:

Zum Prüfplan : Da in der Cross-over Studie zwei Sequenzen vorgesehen sind, sollte die Anzahl der Prüfungsteilnehmer durch 2 teilbar sein (24 oder 26).
Die Ethik-Kommission ersucht administrativ zu klären, ob Prof. Zeitlhofer als Prüfarzt fungieren kann (Pensionierung, Emeritierung,...).

Zur Patienteninformation : Das Wort „Parameter" ist durch einen laienverständlichen Ausdruck zu ersetzen.
Punkt 2: Das Studiendesign ist zu erwähnen (cross-over, zufällige Zuteilung zu einer der beiden Gruppen).
Es geht aus der Beschreibung des Studienablaufs nicht hervor, wo die Studiennächte stattfinden (Zu Hause? Wer bringt die Geräte an? Wer weckt die Teilnehmer?).
Das Polysomnographie-Gerät sowie die „Subjektive Einschätzung der Vigilanz auf der KSS" sind zu erklären.
Punkt 3: Der Studiennutzen ist äußerst optimistisch beschrieben, dies ist abzuschwächen.
Punkt 10: Bei vorzeitigem Studienabbruch **muss** ein aliquoter Teil der Aufwandsentschädigung ausbezahlt werden.
Die Telefonnummer von Prof. Zeitlhofer ist nicht mehr aktuell.

Die Ethik-Kommission ersucht die Antragsteller, bei der Wiedervorlage von geänderten Patienteninformationen Versionsbezeichnungen anzugeben und ein Exemplar mit hervorgehobenen Änderungen beizulegen.

Zur Versicherungsbestätigung : nicht erforderlich

Andere :

Nachtrag vom 21. Juli 2011: Die Antragsteller legen am 18.7.11 überarbeitete Unterlagen vor, die von der Ethik-Kommission akzeptiert werden.

Die Ethik-Kommission geht - rechtlich unverbindlich - davon aus, daß es sich um keine klinische Prüfung gemäß AMG/MPG handelt.

Mitgliederliste der Ethik-Kommission (aktueller Stand am Sitzungstag) beiliegend. Mitglieder der Ethik-Kommission, die für diesen Tagesordnungspunkt als befangen anzusehen waren und daher laut Geschäftsordnung an der Entscheidungsfindung/Abstimmung nicht teilgenommen haben: Univ.Prof.Dr. Friedrich Zimprich, Univ.Prof.Dr. Karl Vass

Univ.Prof.Dr. Ernst Singer
Vorsitzender der Kommission

ACHTUNG: Unter Berücksichtigung der „ICH-Guideline for Good Clinical Practice" gilt dieser Beschluß **ein Jahr ab Datum der Ausstellung.** Gegebenenfalls hat der Antragsteller eine Verlängerung der Gültigkeit mittels Formular für „Meldungen" rechtzeitig vorzulegen.

Ek-Nr: 622/2011   2/2   21.07.11

Figure A.2: The second page of the final vote of the ethics committee concerning our study.

Untersuchung von Wachsamkeit anhand EEG *Version 1.1 vom 11.07.2011*

Probandeninformation und Einwilligungserklärung zur Teilnahme an der klinischen Studie

Eine explorative prospektive Studie zur Untersuchung von Wachsamkeit anhand EEG

Sehr geehrte Teilnehmerin, sehr geehrter Teilnehmer!

Wir laden Sie ein an der oben genannten klinischen Studie teilzunehmen. Die Aufklärung darüber erfolgt in einem ausführlichen Gespräch.

Ihre Teilnahme an dieser klinischen Prüfung erfolgt freiwillig. Sie können jederzeit ohne Angabe von Gründen aus der Studie ausscheiden. Die Ablehnung der Teilnahme oder ein vorzeitiges Ausscheiden aus dieser Studie hat keine nachteiligen Folgen für Ihre medizinische Betreuung.

Klinische Studien sind notwendig, um verlässliche neue medizinische Forschungsergebnisse zu gewinnen. Unverzichtbare Voraussetzung für die Durchführung einer klinischen Studie ist jedoch, dass Sie Ihr Einverständnis zur Teilnahme an dieser klinischen Studie schriftlich erklären. Bitte lesen Sie den folgenden Text als Ergänzung zum Informationsgespräch mit Ihrem Arzt sorgfältig durch und zögern Sie nicht Fragen zu stellen.

Bitte unterschreiben Sie die Einwilligungserklärung nur

- wenn Sie Art und Ablauf der klinischen Studie vollständig verstanden haben,
- wenn Sie bereit sind, der Teilnahme zuzustimmen und
- wenn Sie sich über Ihre Rechte als Teilnehmer an dieser klinischen Studie im klaren sind.

Zu dieser klinischen Studie, sowie zur Probandeninformation und Einwilligungserklärung wurde von der zuständigen Ethikkommission eine befürwortende Stellungnahme abgegeben.

1. Was ist der Zweck der klinischen Studie?

Der Zweck dieser klinischen Studie ist es, Messgrößen zu überprüfen und zu verbessern, die die Schlafqualität und die Tagesaufmerksamkeit beschreiben. Es wird vermutet, dass diese Messwerte besser geeignet sind Schlaf und Aufmerksamkeit zu beschreiben, als das bestehende Verfahren können. Dies gilt es zu überprüfen.

Die beschriebenen Messgrößen basieren auf Biosignalen (Messwerte des menschlichen Körpers) wie dem EEG (Hirnströme), EOG (Augenbewegungen) und dem EMG (Muskelsignale).

Seite 1 von 9

Untersuchung von Wachsamkeit anhand EEG *Version 1.1 vom 11.07.2011*

2. Wie läuft die klinische Studie ab?

Diese klinische Studie wird an mehreren Orten durchgeführt, und es werden insgesamt *26* Personen daran teilnehmen.

Ihre Teilnahme an dieser klinischen Studie wird voraussichtlich zwei mal 24 Stunden dauern. In der Woche vor der ersten Einheit und in der Zeit zwischen den Einheiten füllen Sie jeden Morgen den Fragebogen in Abbildung 1 aus.

<u>Folgende Maßnahmen werden ausschließlich aus Studiengründen durchgeführt:</u>

Bereits eine Woche vor der ersten Einheit beginnen Sie ein Schlaftagebuch zu führen. Das bedeutet, Sie füllen täglich den in Abbildung 1 abgebildeten Fragebogen aus. Dies machen Sie jeden Tag nach dem Aufstehen bis zum Ende der zweiten Einheit, also ungefähr 14 Tage lang.

Die beiden Einheiten werden mit einem Abstand von ungefähr einer Woche durchgeführt, mit einem Abstand von mindestens drei Tagen und maximal 14 Tagen.

Die folgende 24h Einheit, bestehend aus einer Nacht und dem darauffolgenden Tag, wird zwei Mal durchgeführt, einmal mit früherem Aufwecken, einmal mit normal langem Schlaf. Sie werden vor Teilnahme an der Studie gebeten ihre normale Schlafdauer anzugeben. In der Einheit mit kürzerem Schlaf werden sie nach der Hälfte ihrer normalen Schlafdauer geweckt.

Es gibt zwei Gruppen von Studienteilnehmern („Cross-Over-Studie"). Bei der einen Gruppe findet zuerst die Nacht mit früherem Aufstehen statt und danach die Nacht mit normal langem Schlaf, bei der anderen Gruppe ist es umgekehrt. Sie werden zufällig einer Gruppe zugeordnet.

Die Uhrzeiten unten sind Beispiele, falls jemand normalerweise 8 Stunden schläft und 23:00 zu Bett geht.

- Abend (22.00)
  - Anbringen der EEG-, EOG- und EMG-Klebeelektroden des Polysomnographie-Geräts.
  - Anlegen des Aktigraphie-Gerätes (wie eine Armbanduhr).
  - Subjektive Einschätzung der Vigilanz auf der Karolinska Sleepiness Scale (KSS)
  - Durchführen eines Reaktionszeittest. Bei diesem Test müssen Sie gleichzeitig auf eine Farbänderung auf einem Laptopbildschirm und einen Piepston reagieren und eine Taste drücken. Dabei werden die Reaktionszeit und die Korrektheit des Tastendrucks gemessen. Der Test dauert ungefähr 4 Minuten.

Seite 2 von 9

Untersuchung von Wachsamkeit anhand EEG *Version 1.1 vom 11.07.2011*

- Abend (23.00)
  - Zu Bett gehen.
- Morgen
Einheit mit wenig Schlaf 03.00
Einheit mit ausreichend Schlaf 07.00
  - Ausfüllen des Selbstbeurteilungsbogens für Schlaf- und Aufwachqualität.
- Tag
Wiederholung alle 60 Minuten
  - Subjektive Einschätzung der Vigilanz auf der KSS.
  - Reaktionszeittest.
- Nach Bedarf
  - Logbuch Eintrag bei besonderen Vorkommnissen.
- Abend (22.00)
  - Abnahme der EEG-, EOG- und EMG-Klebeelektroden.
  - Ablegen des Aktigraphie-Geräts.
- Ende der 24-Stunden Einheit.

Die beiden Nächte verbringen Sie bei sich zu Hause. Jeweils am Abend vor der Nacht werden durch einen geschulten Studienmitarbeiter die Geräte angelegt. Das Aktigraphie-Gerät hat die Form einer Armbanduhr und wird am Handgelenk getragen. Die Biosignale werden mit einem Gerät der Firma EMBLA aufgezeichnet, das am Körper getragen wird. An diesem Gerät werden Klebeelektroden angeschlossen. Zur Messung des EEGs werden auf der Kopfhaut sechs Elektroden angebracht, zur Messung des EOGs neben den Augen zwei Elektroden und zur Messung des EMGs zwei Elektrode unter dem Kinn, sowie zwei Referenzelektroden und eine neutrale Elektrode.

Bei der Nacht mit früherem Aufstehen müssen Sie selbst dafür sorgen, dass Sie aufwachen, zum Beispiel mit Hilfe eines lauten Weckers.

Die beiden Tage sollen Sie jeweils in einer ruhigen Umgebung verbringen, zum Beispiel ihrer Wohnung. Dabei sollen sie nach dem Frühstück Tätigkeiten wie Lesen, Büroarbeit oder Lernen ausführen. Gegen Mittag sollen Sie ein Mittagessen einnehmen und sich anschließend eine Stunde ausruhen. Dies bedeutet nicht zwangsläufig einen Mittagsschlaf zu halten. Am Nachmittag sollen Sie ebenfalls Tätigkeiten wie Lesen, Büroarbeit oder Lernen nachgehen.

Seite 3 von 9

Untersuchung von Wachsamkeit anhand EEG *Version 1.1 vom 11.07.2011*

Keinesfalls sollten sie körperlich anstrengende Tätigkeiten wie Sport ausführen, die würde die Qualität der Messung negativ beeinflussen.

Dieser Tagesplan ist eine grobe Richtlinie an die Sie sich halten sollen, aber nicht müssen. Jegliche Tätigkeiten am Tag müssen Sie jedoch in einem „Logbuch" vermerken. Das bedeutet einen Eintrag mit Uhrzeit und einer stichwortartiger Beschreibung der Tätigkeit zu machen. Beispielsweise folgende Tätigkeiten müssen vermerkt werden:

- Essen
- Trinken (Kaffee, Tee, Energydrinks)
- Beginn und Ende von sonstigen Tätigkeiten, z.B.
Einkaufen,
Spaziergang,
Lesen,
Lernen,
Büroarbeit,
Fernsehen.

Während dem Folgetag ist vorgesehen, dass Sie ihre Schläfrigkeit stündlich auf der Karolinska Sleepiness Scale einschätzen. Dieser Fragebogen sieht wie folgt aus:

Bitte bewerten Sie Ihre Müdigkeit in den letzten 10 Minuten, indem Sie den Kreis vor der entsprechenden Zahl markieren. Benutzen Sie auch die Zwischenstufen.

1 sehr wach
2
3 wach
4
5 weder wach noch müde
6
7 müde, aber keine Probleme wach zu bleiben
8
9 sehr müde, große Probleme wach zu bleiben, mit dem Schlaf kämpfend

Seite 4 von 9

Figure A.3: The informed consent document (1-4).

Untersuchung von Wachsamkeit anhand EEG *Version 1.1 vom 11.07.2011*

3. **Worin liegt der Nutzen einer Teilnahme an der Klinischen Studie?**

Es ist nicht zu erwarten, dass Sie aus Ihrer Teilnahme an dieser klinischen Studie gesundheitlichen Nutzen ziehen werden.

Der allgemeine wissenschaftliche Nutzen der Studie besteht darin, dass die Ergebnisse dabei helfen können, Schlaf und Tagesschläfrigkeit bzw. -aufmerksamkeit besser messbar und besser kontrollierbar zu machen. Damit könnten einerseits bei Schlafkrankeiten bessere Diagnosen gestellt werden, andererseits könnte die Sicherheit in speziellen Berufsfeldern erhöht werden. Man denke an den Sekundenschlaf eines LKW-Fahrers oder das Einnicken eines Fluglotsen.

4. **Gibt es Risiken, Beschwerden und Begleiterscheinungen?**

Bei einer der beiden 24h Stunden Einheiten werden Sie nach der Hälfte ihrer normalen Schafdauer geweckt und müssen bis zum Abend dieses Tages wach bleiben. Da Sie in dieser Nacht weniger als üblich schlafen, sind Sie an diesem verlängerten Tag wahrscheinlich müder als sonst und somit in Ihrer Reaktionsfähigkeit eingeschränkt. Wir möchten Sie daher auffordern, an diesem Tag keine Tätigkeiten auszuführen, bei denen sich diese Übermüdung negativ auswirken könnte, dies betrifft insbesondere keine Kraftfahrzeuge zu lenken.

Weiters ist zu anzumerken, dass möglicherweise durch die Klebeelektroden leichte lokale Hautirritationen am Kopf entstehen können.

5. **Zusätzliche Einnahme von Arzneimitteln?**

Für die Durchführung der Studie ist keine Einnahme von Arzneimitteln notwendig.

6. **Hat die Teilnahme an der klinischen Studie sonstige Auswirkungen auf die Lebensführung und welche Verpflichtungen ergeben sich daraus?**

Eine 24h Einheit dauert eine Nacht und einen Tag.

Bereits eine Woche vor der ersten Einheit führen Sie ein Schlaftagebuch. Bis zum Ende der zweiten Einheit füllen sie jeden Morgen den Fragebogen in Abbildung 1 aus.

Am Tag vorher und am Tag der Messung trinken Sie bitte keinen Alkohol.

Bei einer der beiden 24 Stunden Einheiten werden Sie früher als gewöhnlich geweckt. Am Folgetag sollen Sie aufgrund der erhöhten Müdigkeit auf Tätigkeiten die uneingeschränkte Aufmerksamkeit benötigen (z.B. Autofahren) verzichten!

7. **Was ist zu tun beim Auftreten von Symptomen, Begleiterscheinungen und/oder Verletzungen?**

Sollten im Verlauf der klinischen Studie irgendwelche Symptome, Begleiterscheinungen oder Verletzungen auftreten, müssen Sie diese Ihrem Studienleiter mitteilen, bei

Seite 6 von 9

Untersuchung von Wachsamkeit anhand EEG *Version 1.1 vom 11.07.2011*

schwerwiegenden Begleiterscheinungen umgehend, ggf. telefonisch (Telefonnummern, etc. siehe unten).

8. **Wann wird die klinische Studie vorzeitig beendet?**

Sie können jederzeit auch ohne Angabe von Gründen, Ihre Teilnahmebereitschaft widerrufen und aus der klinischen Studie ausscheiden ohne dass Ihnen dadurch irgendwelche Nachteile entstehen.

Ihr Studienleiter wird Sie über alle neuen Erkenntnisse, die in Bezug auf diese klinische Studie bekannt werden, und für Sie wesentlich werden könnten, umgehend informieren. Auf dieser Basis können Sie dann Ihre Entscheidung zur **weiteren** Teilnahme an dieser klinischen Studie neu überdenken.

Es ist aber auch möglich, dass Ihr Studienleiter entscheidet, Ihre Teilnahme an der klinischen Studie vorzeitig zu beenden, ohne vorher Ihr Einverständnis einzuholen. Die Gründe hierfür können sein:

a) Sie können den Erfordernissen der Klinischen Studie nicht entsprechen;
b) Ihr Studienleiter hat den Eindruck, dass eine weitere Teilnahme an der klinischen Studie nicht in Ihrem Interesse ist;

9. **In welcher Weise werden die im Rahmen dieser klinischen Studie gesammelten Daten verwendet?**

Sofern gesetzlich nicht etwas anderes vorgesehen ist, haben nur die Prüfer und deren Mitarbeiter Zugang zu den vertraulichen Daten, in denen Sie namentlich genannt werden. Diese Personen unterliegen der Schweigepflicht.

Die Weitergabe der Daten erfolgt ausschließlich zu statistischen Zwecken und Sie werden ausnahmslos darin nicht namentlich genannt. Auch in etwaigen Veröffentlichungen der Daten dieser klinischen Studie werden Sie nicht namentlich genannt.

10. **Entstehen für die Teilnehmer Kosten? Gibt es einen Kostenersatz oder eine Vergütung?**

Durch Ihre Teilnahme an dieser klinischen Studie entstehen für Sie keine zusätzlichen Kosten.

Für Ihre Teilnahme an dieser klinischen Studie erhalten Sie eine Vergütung. Sie erhalten als Entschädigung für Ihren Zeitaufwand (2 mal 24 Stunden) **150 Euro**, wenn Sie sich an die Angaben im Protokoll (z.B. Aufstehen um 03.00, notieren von Ereignissen, etc) halten. Bei vorzeitigem Studienabbruch wird ein aliquoter Anteil der Aufwandsentschädigung ausbezahlt.

11. **Möglichkeit zur Diskussion weiterer Fragen**

Für weitere Fragen im Zusammenhang mit dieser klinischen Studie stehen Ihnen Ihr Studienleiter und seine Mitarbeiter gern zur Verfügung. Auch Fragen, die Ihre Rechte als

Seite 7 von 9

Untersuchung von Wachsamkeit anhand EEG *Version 1.1 vom 11.07.2011*

Patient und Teilnehmer an dieser klinischen Studie betreffen, werden Ihnen gerne beantwortet.

Name der Kontaktperson: Univ.-Professor DDr. Josef Zeitlhofer

Ständig erreichbar unter: +43 699 1065 8660

Name der Kontaktperson: Ao.Univ.-Prof. Dipl.-Ing. Dr. Georg Dorffner

Ständig erreichbar unter: +43 1 40160 36316

Name der Kontaktperson: Dipl.-Ing. Gregor König

Ständig erreichbar unter: +43 650 4563644

12. **Einwilligungserklärung**

Name des Probanden in Druckbuchstaben: ....

Geb. Datum: .... Code: ....

Ich erkläre mich bereit, an der klinischen Studie „Eine explorative prospektive Studie zur Untersuchung von Wachsamkeit anhand EEG" teilzunehmen.

Ich bin von einer der Kontaktpersonen ausführlich und verständlich über „Eine explorative prospektive Studie zur Untersuchung von Wachsamkeit anhand EEG", mögliche Belastungen und Risiken, sowie über Wesen, Bedeutung und Tragweite der klinischen Studie, sich für mich daraus ergebenden Anforderungen aufgeklärt worden. Ich habe darüber hinaus den Text dieser Probandenaufklärung und Einwilligungserklärung, die insgesamt 9 Seiten umfasst gelesen. Aufgetretene Fragen wurden mir vom Studienleiter verständlich und genügend beantwortet. Ich hatte ausreichend Zeit, mich zu entscheiden. Ich habe zurzeit keine weiteren Fragen mehr.

Ich werde den ärztlichen Anordnungen, die für die Durchführung der klinischen Studie erforderlich sind, Folge leisten, behalte mir jedoch das Recht vor, meine freiwillige Mitwirkung jederzeit zu beenden, ohne dass mir daraus Nachteile für meine weitere medizinische Betreuung entstehen.

Ich bin zugleich damit einverstanden, dass meine im Rahmen dieser klinischen Studie ermittelten Daten aufgezeichnet werden. Um die Richtigkeit der Datenaufzeichnung zu überprüfen, dürfen Beauftragte des Auftraggebers und der zuständigen Behörden beim Studienleiter Einblick in meine personenbezogenen Krankheitsdaten nehmen.

Beim Umgang mit den Daten werden die Bestimmungen des Datenschutzgesetzes beachtet.

Eine Kopie dieser Probandeninformation und Einwilligungserklärung habe ich erhalten. Das Original verbleibt beim Studienleiter.

Seite 8 von 9

Untersuchung von Wachsamkeit anhand EEG *Version 1.1 vom 11.07.2011*

....

(Datum und Unterschrift des Probanden)

....

(Datum, Name und Unterschrift der verantwortlichen Kontaktperson)

(Der Patient erhält eine unterschriebene Kopie der Probandeninformation und Einwilligungserklärung, das Original verbleibt im Studienordner des Studienleiters.)

Seite 9 von 9

Figure A.4: The informed consent document (6-9).

Figure A.5: The Pittsburgh Sleep Quality Index form.

(SSA, Saletu et al.)

SCHLAFQUALITÄT	nein	etwas	mäßig	sehr
1. Haben Sie gut geschlafen?				
2. War Ihr Schlaf tief?				
3. Hatten Sie Einschlafschwierigkeiten?				
4. Hatten Sie Durchschlafschwierigkeiten?				
5. Haben Sie schlecht geträumt?				
6. War bei nächtlichem Erwachen das Wiedereinschlafen erschwert?				
7. Wachten Sie frühzeitig auf?				

AUFWACHQUALITÄT	nein	etwas	mäßig	sehr
8. Fühlten Sie sich nach dem Aufstehen benommen?				
9. Waren Sie desorientiert?				
10. Empfanden Sie Müdigkeit?				
11. Waren Sie bei guter Stimmung?				
12. Fühlten Sie sich teilnahmsvoll?				
13. Fühlten Sie sich verlangsamt?				
14. War Ihre Aufmerksamkeit/Konzentration vermindert?				
15. Empfanden Sie Ihren Schlaf als erholsam und erfrischend?				

KÖRPERLICHE BESCHWERDEN	nein	etwas	mäßig	sehr
16. Empfanden Sie Übelkeit?				
17. Hatten Sie Kopfschmerzen?				
18 Empfanden Sie Mundtrockenheit?				
19. Bemerkten Sie Schwindelgefühle?				
20. Waren Ihre Bewegungen unkoordiniert?				

22. Wann gingen Sie zu Bett?   _____ h _____ min.

23. Wann drehten Sie das Licht aus?   _____ h _____ min.

24. Wann schliefen Sie ein?   _____ h _____ min.

25. Wie oft erwachten Sie nachts?   _____ mal

26. Wann erwachten Sie zuletzt morgens?   _____ h _____ min.

27. Wieviel Schlaf hatten Sie insgesamt?   _____ Std. _____ min.

28. *Wann verließen Sie das Bett?*   _____ h _____ min.

Figure A.6: The sleep- and wakeup-quality self-assessment form, Saletu et al (1987).

Nomenclature

AASM American Academy of Sleep Medicine

BCI Brain Computer Interfaces

BSS Blind Source Separation

CNS Central Nervous System

ECoG Electrocorticogram

EEG Electroencephalography

EMG Electromyogram

EOG Electrooculogram

EPSP Excitatory post-synaptic potential

ERP Even-related Potentials

ESS Epworth Sleepiness Scale

fMRI functional Magnetic Resonance Imaging

HRV Heart Rate Variability

IPSP Inhibitory post-synaptic potential

KDS Karolinska Drowsiness Score

KSS Karolinska Sleepiness Scale

LCCS Limited Capacity Control System

MSLT Multiple Sleep Latency Test

MWT Maintenance of Wakefulness Test

PCT Psychomotor Vigilance Test

PEI Permutation Entropy Index

PET Positron Emission Tomography

PNS Peripheral Nervous System

PSD Power Spectral Density

RTT Reaction Time Test

SD Sleep Deprivation

SE Standard Error of the Mean/Median

SEM Slow Eye Movements

SSS Stanford Sleepiness Scale

SSVEP Steady-State Visual Evoked Potentials

List of Figures

2.1	A typical neuron.	11
2.2	Recording of brain activity.	17
2.3	Early recording of a human EEG.	20
2.4	The 10-20 electrode placement system.	21
2.5	A Wireless EEG Neuro-Headset.	23
2.6	EOG recording.	27
2.7	The classical EEG frequency bands.	31
2.8	The Permutation Entropy Index.	36
2.9	LORETA - EEG forward problem.	40
3.1	The 3 process model of daytime alertness and sleepiness.	54
3.2	Example of an actigram	57
3.3	Siesta Group Reaction Time Test	61
3.4	Steering Wheel Angle. Raw, High-pass filtered, and standard deviation.	65
4.1	Actigraphy, Sleep diary, and Recording sessions.	87
4.2	Time schedule of recording session.	89
4.3	Cambridge Neurotechnology Actiwatch	91

LIST OF FIGURES

4.4   Location of the EEG electrodes. 95

4.5   EEG data preprocessing. 99

4.6   Spectral Edge Frequency 106

4.7   Example of a raw fragmented EEG variable. 108

4.8   Example of the aggregation of the raw EEG data using the median values per slice. 108

4.9   Example of a normalized aggregated trend of an EEG-based variable. . . 109

4.10 Example of the aggregation of individual daytime trends to a general model. 110

4.11 Normalized patterns to detect circadian trends. 113

4.12 Classification of sessions. 116

5.1   Subjects' sleep quality 121

5.2   Example of Sleep Diary Data 122

5.3   The homeostatic property of EOG artifacts. 126

5.4   The homeostatic property of the relative beta power. 126

5.5   The homeostatic property of the high alpha power 127

5.6   The theta factor as example for concave circadian behavior. 128

5.7   The concave circadian behavior of the low alpha activity. 130

5.8   The convex circadian behavior of the KSS. 130

5.9   The convex circadian behavior of theta pauses 131

5.10 KSS vs. simulation of sleepiness. 133

5.11 Theta events vs. simulation of alertness. 134

5.12 Separation of sessions based on the relative theta power. 136

5.13 Separation of sessions based on artifacts with relative high frequency. . . 136

LIST OF FIGURES

5.14 Separation of sessions based on relative beta power. 137

5.15 Separation of sessions based on the SEF95. 137

5.16 Example classification using relative that power. 140

5.17 Example classification using the $(\theta + \alpha)/\beta$ ratio. 140

6.1 The homeostatic property of rapid eye movements derived from the EOG. 144

6.2 The homeostatic property of slow eye movements derived from the EOG. 145

A.1 Vote of the ethics committee 1 154

A.2 Vote of the ethics committee 2 155

A.3 The informed consent document (1-4). 156

A.4 The informed consent document (6-9). 157

A.5 The Pittsburgh Sleep Quality Index form. 158

A.6 The sleep- and wakeup-quality self-assessment form, Saletu et al (1987). . 159

List of Tables

3.1	Summary of the reported trends of EEG features.	76
4.1	Fraction of artifact types.	100
4.2	Definition of the EEG frequency bands.	103
5.1	Ranking of homeostatic trends after normal sleep and sleep deprivation.	124
5.2	Ranking of the homeostatic trends of the model of all sessions.	125
5.3	Ranking of variables' circadian trends following a concave and convex pattern.	129
5.4	Ranking for the 3-process model.	132
5.5	Separability ranking.	135
5.6	Normal sessions classification ranking.	138
5.7	Sleep deprived session classification ranking.	139
5.8	Classification ranking.	139
5.9	Ranking of combined classification.	141

LIST OF TABLES

Bibliography

[1] *Medical Devices and Systems (The Biomedical Engineering Handbook)*. CRC, 1 edition, Apr. 2006.

[2] N. Abramson. Information theory and coding. 1963.

[3] P. Achermann and A. A. Borbély. Simulation of daytime vigilance by the additive interaction of a homeostatic and a circadian process. *Biological cybernetics*, 71(2):115–21, Jan. 1994.

[4] E. Adrian. The Berger rhythm: potential changes from the occipital lobes in man. *Brain*, 1934.

[5] D. Aeschbach, J. R. Matthews, T. T. Postolache, M. a. Jackson, H. a. Giesen, and T. a. Wehr. Dynamics of the human EEG during prolonged wakefulness: evidence for frequency-specific circadian and homeostatic influences. *Neuroscience letters*, 239(2-3):121–4, Dec. 1997.

[6] D. Aeschbach, J. R. Matthews, T. T. Postolache, M. A. Jackson, H. A. Giesen, and T. A. Wehr. Two circadian rhythms in the human electroencephalogram during wakefulness. *The American journal of physiology*, 277(6 Pt 2):R1771–9, Dec. 1999.

[7] T. Åkerstedt, S. Folkard, and C. Portin. Predictions from the three-process model of alertness. *Aviation, space, and environmental medicine*, 75(3 Suppl):A75–83, Mar. 2004.

[8] T. Åkerstedt and M. Gillberg. Subjective and objective sleepiness in the active individual. *The International journal of neuroscience*, 52(1-2):29–37, May 1990.

[9] T. Åkerstedt, G. Kecklund, and M. Gillberg. Sleep and sleepiness in relation to stress and displaced work hours. *Physiology & behavior*, 92(1-2):250–5, Sept. 2007.

[10] T. Akerstedt and P. M. Nilsson. Sleep as restitution: an introduction. *Journal of Internal Medicine*, 254(1):6–12, July 2003.

[11] M. Akin, M. B. Kurt, N. Sezgin, and M. Bayram. Estimating vigilance level by using EEG and EMG signals. *Neural Computing and Applications*, 17(3):227–236, May 2007.

[12] T. Altmüller. *Driver monitoring and drowsiness detection by steering signal analysis*. Phd thesis, Universität der Bundeswehr München, 2007.

[13] S. Ancoli-Israel, R. Cole, C. Alessi, M. Chambers, W. Moorcroft, and C. P. Pollak. The role of actigraphy in the study of sleep and circadian rhythms. *Sleep*, 26(3):342–92, May 2003.

[14] S. Ancoli-Israel and T. Roth. Characteristics of insomnia in the United States: results of the 1991 National Sleep Foundation Survey. *Sleep*, 22 Suppl 2:347–353, 1999.

[15] P. Anderer, G. Gruber, S. Parapatics, M. Woertz, T. Miazhynskaia, G. Klösch, B. Saletu, J. Zeitlhofer, M.-J. Barbanoj, H. Danker-Hopfe, S.-L. Himanen, B. Kemp, T. Penzel, M. Grozinger, D. Kunz, P. Rappelsberger, A. Schloegl, and G. Dorffner. An E-health solution for automatic sleep classification according to Rechtschaffen and Kales: validation study of the Somnolyzer 24 x 7 utilizing the Siesta database. *Neuropsychobiology*, 51(3):115–133, Jan. 2005.

[16] P. Anderer, G. Klösch, G. Gruber, E. Trenker, R. D. Pascual-Marqui, J. Zeitlhofer, M.-J. Barbanoj, P. Rappelsberger, and B. Saletu. Low-resolution brain electromagnetic tomography revealed simultaneously active frontal and parietal sleep spindle sources in the human cortex. *Neuroscience*, 103(3):581–92, Jan. 2001.

[17] A. Anund, G. Kecklund, A. Vadeby, M. Hjälmdahl, and T. Åkerstedt. The alerting effect of hitting a rumble strip–a simulator study with sleepy drivers. *Accident; analysis and prevention*, 40(6):1970–6, Nov. 2008.

[18] M. Atienza, J. L. Cantero, R. Stickgold, and J. A. Hobson. Eyelid movements measured by Nightcap predict slow eye movements during quiet wakefulness in humans. *Journal of sleep research*, 13(1):25–9, Mar. 2004.

[19] M. Avidan, L. Zhang, and B. Burnside. Anesthesia awareness and the bispectral index. *England Journal of*, pages 1097–1108, 2008.

[20] C. Bandt and B. Pompe. Permutation entropy: a natural complexity measure for time series. *Physical review letters*, 88(17):174102, Apr. 2002.

[21] H. Berger. Über das Elektrenkephalogramm des Menschen. *European Archives of Psychiatry and Clinical*, 1929.

[22] M. Birbaumer, V. Braitenberg, and H. Brinkmeier. *Neuro-und Sinnesphysiologie*. Springer Verlag, 5th editio edition, 2006.

[23] N. Birbaumer. Breaking the silence: brain-computer interfaces (BCI) for communication and motor control. *Psychophysiology*, 43(6):517–32, Nov. 2006.

[24] R. Bishel, J. Coleman, and R. Lorenz. Lane Departure Warning for CVO in the USA. *Society of Automotive*, 1998.

[25] A. A. Borbély. A two process model of sleep regulation. *Human neurobiology*, 1(3):195–204, Jan. 1982.

[26] J. D. Bronzino. *Biomedical Engineering and Instrumentation: Basic Concepts and Applications*. 1986.

[27] J. D. Bronzino. Principles of Electroencephalography. In *Collection*. CRC Press LLC, second edi edition, 2000.

[28] J. B. Brookings, G. F. Wilson, and C. R. Swain. Psychophysiological responses to changes in workload during simulated air traffic control. *Biological Psychology*, 42(3):361–377, Feb. 1996.

[29] A. a. Bruzzo, B. Gesierich, M. Santi, C. A. Tassinari, N. Birbaumer, and G. Rubboli. Permutation entropy to detect vigilance changes and preictal states from scalp EEG in epileptic patients. A preliminary study. *Neurological sciences : official journal of the Italian Neurological Society and of the Italian Society of Clinical Neurophysiology*, 29(1):3–9, Feb. 2008.

[30] S. P. Buckelew, D. E. DeGood, K. D. Roberts, J. D. Butkovic, and A. S. MacKewn. Awake EEG disregulation in good compared to poor sleepers. *Applied psychophysiology and biofeedback*, 34(2):99–103, June 2009.

[31] D. J. Buysse, C. F. Reynolds III, T. H. Monk, S. R. Berman, and D. J. Kupfer. The Pittsburgh sleep quality index: A new instrument for psychiatric practice and research. *Psychiatry Research*, 28(2):193–213, May 1989.

[32] P. P. Caffier, U. Erdmann, and P. Ullsperger. Experimental evaluation of eye-blink parameters as a drowsiness measure. *European Journal of Applied Physiology*, 89(3):319–325, May 2003.

[33] C. Cajochen, D. P. Brunner, K. Kräuchi, P. Graw, and A. Wirz-Justice. Power density in theta/alpha frequencies of the waking EEG progressively increases during sustained wakefulness. *Sleep*, 18(10):890–4, Dec. 1995.

[34] C. Cajochen, V. Knoblauch, K. Kräuchi, C. Renz, and A. Wirz-Justice. Dynamics of frontal EEG activity, sleepiness and body temperature under high and low sleep pressure. *Neuroreport*, 12(10):2277–81, July 2001.

[35] M. Carskadon. Sleep tendency: an objective measure of sleep loss. *Sleep Res*, 1977.

[36] R. Caton. Electrical currents of the brain. *The Journal of Nervous and Mental Disease*, 1875.

[37] H. Cecotti. Spelling with Brain-Computer Interfaces-Current trends and prospects. 2010.

[38] R. Conradt, U. Brandenburg, T. Penzel, and J. Hasan. Vigilance transitions in reaction time test: a method of describing the state of alertness more objectively. *Clinical Neurophysiology*, 1999.

[39] M. Corsi-Cabrera, L. Galindo-Vilchis, Y. Del-Río-Portilla, C. Arce, and J. Ramos-Loyo. Within-subject reliability and inter-session stability of EEG power and coherent activity in women evaluated monthly over nine months. *Clinical neurophysiology : official journal of the International Federation of Clinical Neurophysiology*, 118(1):9–21, Jan. 2007.

[40] A. Cortoos, E. De Valck, M. Arns, M. H. M. Breteler, and R. Cluydts. An exploratory study on the effects of tele-neurofeedback and tele-biofeedback on objective and subjective sleep in patients with primary insomnia. *Applied psychophysiology and biofeedback*, 35(2):125–34, June 2010.

[41] L. Cummings, a. Dane, J. Rhodes, P. Lynch, and a. M. Hughes. Diurnal variation in the quantitative EEG in healthy adult volunteers. *British journal of clinical pharmacology*, 50(1):21–6, July 2000.

[42] P. R. Davidson, R. D. Jones, and M. T. Peiris. EEG-based lapse detection with high temporal resolution. *IEEE transactions on bio-medical engineering*, 54(5):832–839, May 2007.

[43] L. De Gennaro, M. Ferrara, and M. Bertini. The boundary between wakefulness and sleep: quantitative electroencephalographic changes during the sleep onset period. *Neuroscience*, 107(1):1–11, Jan. 2001.

[44] L. De Gennaro, M. Ferrara, G. Curcio, and R. Cristiani. Antero-posterior EEG changes during the wakefulness-sleep transition. *Clinical Neurophysiology*, 112(10):1901–11, 2001.

[45] L. De Gennaro, M. Ferrara, F. Ferlazzo, and M. Bertini. Slow eye movements and EEG power spectra during wake-sleep transition. *Clinical Neurophysiology*, 111(12):2107–2115, Dec. 2000.

[46] L. De Gennaro, F. Vecchio, M. Ferrara, G. Curcio, P. Rossini, and C. Babiloni. Changes in fronto-posterior functional coupling at sleep onset in humans. *Journal of sleep research*, 13(3):209–217, 2004.

[47] B. Desai, S. Whitman, and D. A. Bouffard. The role of the EEG in epilepsy of long duration. *Epilepsia*, 29(5):601–6.

[48] D. Dinges, M. Mallis, and G. Maislin. Evaluation of techniques for ocular measurement as an index of fatigue and the basis for alertness management. Technical Report April, 1998.

[49] R. Downey and M. H. Bonnet. Performance during frequent sleep disruption. *Sleep*, 10(4):354–63, 1987.

[50] J. Dudel. Innerneurale Homöostase und Kommunikation, Erregung. *Neuro-und Sinnesphysiologie*, 2006.

[51] J. Enderle. Introduction to biomedical engineering. 2011.

[52] C. Fabian, M. Fuller, B. Guo, and X. Lin. Development of an Electro-Oculography (EOG) Measurement System. *Report, Vestibular*, pages 1–12, 2002.

[53] E. Fetz. Operant conditioning of specific patterns of neural and muscular activity. *Science*, 1971.

[54] L. a. Finelli, H. Baumann, a. a. Borbély, and P. Achermann. Dual electroencephalogram markers of human sleep homeostasis: correlation between theta activity in waking and slow-wave activity in sleep. *Neuroscience*, 101(3):523–9, Jan. 2000.

[55] A. Flexer, G. Gruber, and G. Dorffner. A reliable probabilistic sleep stager based on a single EEG signal. *Artificial intelligence in medicine*, 33(3):199–207, Mar. 2005.

[56] N. Freedman. *Determinants and Measurements of Daytime Sleepiness*. 2007.

[57] F. G. Freeman, P. J. Mikulka, M. W. Scerbo, and L. Scott. An evaluation of an adaptive automation system using a cognitive vigilance task. *Biol Psychiatry*, 67(3):283–97, 2004.

[58] K. Gabrielsen. *Drowsy drivers, steering data, and random processes*. 1995.

[59] M. Gillberg, G. Kecklund, and T. Åkerstedt. Relations between performance and subjective ratings of sleepiness during a night awake. *Sleep*, 17(3):236–41, Apr. 1994.

[60] M. Gillberg, G. Kecklund, and T. Åkerstedt. Sleepiness and performance of professional drivers in a truck simulator–comparisons between day and night driving. *Journal of sleep research*, 5(1):12–5, Mar. 1996.

[61] B. Graimann, B. Allison, and G. Pfurtscheller. Brain–Computer Interfaces: A Gentle Introduction. *Brain-Computer Interfaces*, pages 1–27, 2010.

[62] Gray. *Entropy and information theory*. Springer, New York, 1990.

[63] S. Gudmundsson, T. P. Runarsson, S. Sigurdsson, G. Eiriksdottir, and K. Johnsen. Reliability of quantitative EEG features. *Clinical Neurophysiology*, 118(10):2162–71, Oct. 2007.

[64] A. Guggisberg, J. Mathis, U. Herrmann, and C. Hess. The functional relationship between yawning and vigilance. *Behav Brain Res*, 179(1):159–166, 2007.

[65] C. Guilleminault. Sleep and Alertness: Chronobiological, Behavioral, and Medical Aspects of Napping. *JAMA: The Journal of the American Medical Association*, 263(16):2255–2255, Apr. 1990.

[66] M. Haenggi, H. Ypparila, J. Takala, I. Korhonen, M. Luginb{ü}hl, S. Petersen-Felix, and S. M. Jakob. Measuring Depth of Sedation with Auditory Evoked Potentials During Controlled Infusion of Propofol and Remifentanil in Healthy Volunteers. *Anesthesia and Analgesia*, 99(6):1728–1736, 2004.

[67] S. Hanke, J. Zeitlhofer, G. Wiest, and W. Mayr. Automated Vigilance Classification based on EOG signals: Preliminary Results. *World Congress on Medical Physics and Biomedical Engineering*, 2009.

[68] E. Hoddes, V. Zarcone, H. Smythe, R. Phillips, and W. C. Dement. Quantification of Sleepiness: A New Approach. *Psychophysiology*, 10(4):431–436, July 1973.

[69] J. Horne. Sleepiness as a need for sleep: when is enough, enough? *Neuroscience and biobehavioral reviews*, 34(1):108–18, Jan. 2010.

[70] B. Jap, S. Lal, P. Fischer, and E. Bekiaris. Using EEG spectral components to assess algorithms for detecting fatigue. *Expert Systems with Applications*, 36(2):2352–2359, Mar. 2009.

[71] R. R. Johnson, D. P. Popovic, R. E. Olmstead, M. Stikic, D. J. Levendowski, and C. Berka. Drowsiness/alertness algorithm development and validation using synchronized EEG and cognitive performance to individualize a generalized model. *Biological psychology*, 87(2):241–50, May 2011.

[72] K. Kaida, M. Takahashi, T. Åkerstedt, A. Nakata, Y. Otsuka, T. Haratani, and K. Fukasawa. Validation of the Karolinska sleepiness scale against performance and EEG variables. *Clinical Neurophysiology*, 117(7):1574–81, July 2006.

[73] D. Kaiser. Ultradian and Circadian Effects in Electroencephalography Activity. *Biofeedback*, 36(4):148–151, 2008.

[74] S. Kelley. *Monitoring level of consciousness during anesthesia and sedation. A Clinician's Guide to the Bispectral Index.* 2003.

[75] M. Kendall. A new measure of rank correlation. *Biometrika*, 1938.

[76] P. Kennedy. Restoration of neural output from a paralyzed patient by a direct brain connection. *Neuroreport*, 1998.

[77] M. K. Kiymik, M. Akin, and A. Subasi. Automatic recognition of alertness level by using wavelet transform and artificial neural network. *Journal of neuroscience methods*, 139(2):231–40, Oct. 2004.

[78] G. H. Klem, H. O. Lüders, H. H. Jasper, and C. Elger. The ten-twenty electrode system of the International Federation. The International Federation of Clinical Neurophysiology. *Electroencephalography and clinical neurophysiology. Supplement*, 52:3–6, Jan. 1999.

[79] G. Klösch, B. Kemp, T. Penzel, A. Schlogl, P. Rappelsberger, E. Trenker, G. Gruber, J. Zeitlhofer, B. Saletu, W. M. Herrmann, S.-L. Himanen, D. Kunz, M.-J. Barbanoj, J. Roschke, A. Varri, and G. Dorffner. The SIESTA project polygraphic and clinical database. *IEEE Engineering in Medicine and Biology Magazine*, 20(3):51–57, 2001.

[80] C. Koch and N. Tsuchiya. Attention and consciousness: two distinct brain processes. *Trends in cognitive sciences*, 11(1):16–22, Jan. 2007.

[81] J. Kropotov. *Quantitative EEG, Event-Related Potentials and Neurotherapy.* Academic Press, 2008.

[82] A. Kumar and S. Anand. A depth of anaesthesia index from linear regression of EEG parameters. *Journal of clinical monitoring and computing*, 20(2):67–73, Apr. 2006.

[83] S. Lal and a. Craig. A critical review of the psychophysiology of driver fatigue. *Biological psychology*, 55(3):173–94, Feb. 2001.

[84] S. Lal, A. Craig, P. Boord, L. Kirkup, and H. Nguyen. Development of an algorithm for an EEG-based driver fatigue countermeasure. *Journal of Safety Research*, 34(3):321–328, Aug. 2003.

[85] S. K. L. Lal and A. Craig. Driver fatigue: electroencephalography and psychological assessment. *Psychophysiology*, 39(3):313–21, May 2002.

[86] T. Lee-Chiong. New Sleep Scoring Guidelines. *chestnet.org*, 2008.

[87] S. B. Legarda, D. McMahon, S. Othmer, and S. Othmer. Clinical neurofeedback: case studies, proposed mechanism, and implications for pediatric neurology practice. *Journal of child neurology*, 26(8):1045–51, Aug. 2011.

[88] E. C. E. Leuthardt, G. Schalk, J. Roland, A. Rouse, and D. D. W. Moran. Evolution of brain-computer interfaces: going beyond classic motor physiology. *Neurosurgical focus*, 27(1):E4, July 2009.

[89] S. F. Liang, C.-T. Lin, R. C. Wu, Y. C. Chen, T. Y. Huang, and T. P. Jung. Monitoring driver's alertness based on the driving performance estimation and the EEG power spectrum analysis. In *Annual International Conference of the IEEE Engineering in Medicine and Biology Society. IEEE Engineering in Medicine and Biology Society. Conference*, volume 6, pages 5738–41, Jan. 2005.

[90] J. Lim and D. F. Dinges. Sleep deprivation and vigilant attention. *Annals of the New York Academy of Sciences*, 1129:305–22, Jan. 2008.

[91] C.-T. Lin, L.-W. Ko, I.-f. Chung, T.-Y. Huang, Y. C. Chen, T.-P. Jung, and S.-F. Liang. Adaptive EEG-based alertness estimation system by using ICA-based fuzzy neural networks. *Circuits and Systems I: Regular Papers, IEEE Transactions on*, 53(11):2469–2476, 2006.

[92] C.-T. Lin, R. Wu, T.-P. Jung, S.-F. Liang, and T.-Y. Huang. Estimating driving performance based on EEG spectrum analysis. *EURASIP Journal on Applied Signal Processing*, 2005:3165–3174, 2005.

[93] D. Lindsley. *Attention, consciousness, sleep and wakefulness*. 1960.

[94] N. Lofthouse, L. E. Arnold, S. Hersch, E. Hurt, and R. Debeus. A review of neurofeedback treatment for pediatric ADHD. *Journal of attention disorders*, 16(5):351–72, July 2012.

[95] N. H. Mackworth. The breakdown of vigilance during prolonged visual search. *Quarterly Journal of Experimental Psychology*, 1(1):6–21, Apr. 1948.

[96] N. H. Mackworth. The breakdown of vigilance durning prolonged visual search. *The Quarterly Journal of Experimental Psychology*, 1(1):6–21, Apr. 1948.

[97] S. Makeig and T.-P. Jung. Changes in alertness are a principal component of variance in the EEG spectrum. *Neuroreport*, 7(1):213–6, Dec. 1995.

[98] S. Makeig and T.-P. Jung. Tonic, phasic, and transient EEG correlates of auditory awareness in drowsiness. *Brain research. Cognitive brain research*, 4(1):15–25, July 1996.

[99] S. Makeig, T.-P. Jung, and T. J. Sejnowski. Awareness during drowsiness: dynamics and electrophysiological correlates. *Canadian journal of experimental psychology = Revue canadienne de psychologie expérimentale*, 54(4):266–73, Dec. 2000.

[100] J. Malmivuo. Bioelectromagnetism. *MEDICAL AND BIOLOGICAL ENGINEERING AND*, 1996.

[101] P. Manganotti, a. Palermo, S. Patuzzo, G. Zanette, and a. Fiaschi. Decrease in motor cortical excitability in human subjects after sleep deprivation. *Neuroscience letters*, 304(3):153–6, May 2001.

[102] S. Melamed, U. Ugarten, A. Shirom, L. Kahana, Y. Lerman, and P. Froom. Chronic burnout, somatic arousal and elevated salivary cortisol levels. *Journal of psychosomatic research*, 46(6):591–8, 1999.

[103] E. Michail, A. Kokonozi, I. Chouvarda, and N. Maglaveras. EEG and HRV markers of sleepiness and loss of control during car driving. In *Engineering in Medicine and Biology Society, 2008. EMBS 2008. 30th Annual International Conference of the IEEE*, volume 2008, pages 2566–2569. IEEE, Jan. 2008.

[104] Y. Morad, H. Lemberg, and N. Yofe. Pupillography as an objective indicator of fatigue. *Current Eye Research*, (906380687), 2000.

[105] D. Moran. Evolution of brain-computer interface: action potentials, local field potentials and electrocorticograms. *Current opinion in neurobiology*, 20(6):741–5, Dec. 2010.

[106] D. Moretti, F. Babiloni, F. Carducci, F. Cincotti, E. Remondini, P. Rossini, S. Salinari, and C. Babiloni. Computerized processing of EEG-EOG-EMG artifacts for multi-centric studies in EEG oscillations and event-related potentials. *International Journal of Psychophysiology*, 47(3):199–216, 2003.

[107] F. Morisson. Daytime Sleepiness and EEG Spectral Analysis in Apneic Patients Before and After Treatment With Continuous Positive Airway Pressure. *Chest*, 119(1):45–52, Jan. 2001.

[108] Y. Nam, Q. Zhao, and A. Cichocki. A tongue-machine interface: detection of tongue positions by glossokinetic potentials. *Neural Information Processing.*, 2010.

[109] (National Transportation Safety Board). Evaluation of US Department of Transportation Efforts in the 1990s to Address Operator Fatigue. (May), 1999.

[110] T. Niederl. *Untersuchungen zu kumulativen psychischen und physiologischen Effekten des fliegenden Personals auf der Kurzstrecke*. PhD thesis, 2007.

[111] B. S. Oken, M. C. Salinsky, and S. M. Elsas. Vigilance, alertness, or sustained attention: physiological basis and measurement. *Clinical Neurophysiology*, 117(9):1885–901, 2006.

[112] E. Olofsen, J. W. Sleigh, and A. Dahan. Permutation entropy of the electroencephalogram: a measure of anaesthetic drug effect. *British journal of anaesthesia*, 101(6):810–21, Dec. 2008.

[113] N. R. Pal, C.-Y. Chuang, L.-W. Ko, C.-F. Chao, T.-P. Jung, S.-F. Liang, and C.-T. Lin. EEG-Based Subject- and Session-independent Drowsiness Detection: An Unsupervised Approach. *EURASIP Journal on Advances in Signal Processing*, 2008:1–12, 2008.

[114] C. Papadelis, Z. Chen, C. Kourtidou-Papadeli, P. D. Bamidis, I. Chouvarda, E. Bekiaris, and N. Maglaveras. Monitoring sleepiness with on-board electrophysiological recordings for preventing sleep-deprived traffic accidents. *Clinical Neurophysiology*, 118(9):1906–22, Sept. 2007.

[115] S. Parapatics, B. Saletu, G. Gruber, G. Klösch, P. Anderer, M.-J. Barbanoj, H. Danker-Hopfe, S.-L. Himanen, B. Kemp, T. Penze, J. Röschke, D. Kunz,

J. Zeitlhofer, and G. Dorffner. Europäische Normdaten (SIESTA) zum Selbstbeurteilungsbogen für Schlaf- und Aufwachqualität (SSA). In *ASRA*, Innsbruck, Austria, 2003.

[116] R. Parasuraman. *The attentive brain*. The MIT Press, 2000.

[117] R. D. Pascual-Marqui. Review of methods for solving the EEG inverse problem. *International Journal of Bioelectromagnetism*, 1(1):75–86, 1999.

[118] R. D. Pascual-Marqui. Standardized low-resolution brain electromagnetic tomography (sLORETA): technical details. *Methods and findings in experimental and clinical pharmacology*, 24 Suppl D:5–12, Jan. 2002.

[119] R. D. Pascual-Marqui. Discrete, 3D distributed, linear imaging methods of electric neuronal activity. Part 1: exact, zero error localization. pages 1–16, Oct. 2007.

[120] R. D. Pascual-Marqui, M. Esslen, K. Kochi, and D. Lehmann. Functional imaging with low-resolution brain electromagnetic tomography (LORETA): a review. *Methods and findings in experimental and clinical pharmacology*, 24 Suppl C:91–5, Jan. 2002.

[121] R. D. Pascual-Marqui, C. C. Michel, and D. Lehmann. Low resolution electromagnetic tomography: a new method for localizing electrical activity in the brain. *International Journal of Psychophysiology*, 18(1):49–65, 1994.

[122] M. T. Peiris, R. D. Jones, P. R. Davidson, G. J. Carroll, T. L. Signal, P. J. Parkin, M. van den Berg, and P. J. Bones. Identification of vigilance lapses using EEG/EOG by expert human raters. *Conference proceedings : Annual International Conference of the IEEE Engineering in Medicine and Biology Society IEEE Engineering in Medicine and Biology Society Conference*, 6:5735–5737, 2005.

[123] M. T. R. Peiris, R. D. Jones, P. R. Davidson, and P. J. Bones. Detecting behavioral microsleeps from EEG power spectra. *Conference proceedings : Annual International Conference of the IEEE Engineering in Medicine and Biology Society IEEE Engineering in Medicine and Biology Society Conference*, 1:5723–6, 2006.

[124] N. Pop-Jordanova. Spectrum-weighted EEG frequency ("brain-rate") as a quantitative indicator of mental arousal. *Prilozi*, 42:35–42, 2005.

[125] E. Portouli, E. Bekiaris, V. Papakostopoulos, and N. Maglaveras. On-road experiment for collecting driving behavioural data of sleepy drivers. *Somnologie*, 11(4):259–267, Oct. 2007.

[126] A. Putilov, O. Donskaya, E. Verevkin, and M. Shtark. Structuring the interindividual variation in waking EEG can help to discriminate between the objective markers of sleep debt and sleep pressure. *Somnologie*, 13(2):72–88, June 2009.

[127] R. Rangayyan. *Biomedical signal analysis*. 2002.

[128] C. C. Rao and S. Mitra. Theory and application of constrained inverse of matrices. *SIAM Journal on Applied Mathematics*, 24(4):473–488, 1973.

[129] A. Rechtschaffen and A. Kales. A manual of standardized terminology, techniques and scoring system for sleep stages of human subjects. *US Dept. of Health, Education, and Welfare*, 1968.

[130] P. Ritter, R. Becker, C. Graefe, and A. Villringer. Evaluating gradient artifact correction of EEG data acquired simultaneously with fMRI. *Magnetic resonance imaging*, 25(6):923–32, July 2007.

[131] M. Rohál'ová, P. Sykacek, and M. Koskaand. Detection of the EEG Artifacts by the Means of the (Extended) Kalman Filter. *Measurement Science Review*, 2001.

[132] R. Rosipal, B. Peters, and G. Kecklund. EEG-based drivers' drowsiness monitoring using a hierarchical Gaussian mixture model. *Augmented Cognition, HCII 2007*, pages 294–303, 2007.

[133] G. Ruffini, S. Dunne, E. Farres, I. Cester, P. C. P. Watts, S. Silva, C. Grau, L. Fuentemilla, J. Marco-Pallares, and B. Vandecasteele. ENOBIO dry electrophysiology electrode; first human trial plus wireless electrode system. *Conference proceedings : Annual International Conference of the IEEE Engineering in Medicine and Biology Society IEEE Engineering in Medicine and Biology Society Conference*, 2007:6690–4, 2007.

[134] R. Sangal, L. Thomas, and M. Mitler. Disorders of excessive sleepiness. Treatment improves ability to stay awake but does not reduce sleepiness. *Chest*, 102(3):699–703, Sept. 1992.

[135] J. Santamaria and K. Chiappa. The EEG of drowsiness in normal adults. *Journal of Clinical Neurophysiology*, 4(4):327, 1987.

[136] E. a. Schmidt, M. Schrauf, M. Simon, M. Fritzsche, A. Buchner, and W. E. Kincses. Drivers' misjudgement of vigilance state during prolonged monotonous daytime driving. *Accident; analysis and prevention*, 41(5):1087–93, Sept. 2009.

[137] R. F. Schmidt. Physiologie des Menschen mit Pathophysiologie. *Book*, 2007.

[138] G. Schneider. Detection of awareness in surgical patients with EEG-based indices–bispectral index and patient state index . *British Journal of Anaesthesia*, 91(3):329–335, Sept. 2003.

[139] A. Schultz, M. Siedenberg, U. Grouven, T. Kneif, and B. Schultz. Comparison of Narcotrend Index, Bispectral Index, spectral and entropy parameters during induction of propofol-remifentanil anaesthesia. *Journal of clinical monitoring and computing*, 22(2):103–11, 2008.

[140] L. M. Selwa, M. L. Marzec, R. D. Chervin, K. J. Weatherwax, B. V. Vaughn, N. Foldvary-Schaefer, L. Wang, Y. Song, and B. A. Malow. Sleep staging and respiratory events in refractory epilepsy patients: Is there a first night effect? *Epilepsia*, 49(12):2063–8, 2008.

[141] G. R. Shamsaei. *Review Of Clinical Electroencephalography*. 2010.

[142] C. Shannon. A mathematical theory of communication. Technical report, 1948.

[143] C. E. Shannon. Communication in the Presence of Noise. 3(2), 1998.

[144] A. L. Sharpley, R. A. Solomon, and P. J. Cowen. Evaluation of first night effect using ambulatory monitoring and automatic sleep stage analysis. *Sleep*, 11(3):273–6, 1988.

[145] J. C. Sigl and N. G. Chamoun. An introduction to bispectral analysis for the electroencephalogram. *Journal of clinical monitoring*, 10(6):392–404, 1994.

[146] B. Streitberg, J. Röhmel, W. M. Herrmann, and S. Kubicki. COMSTAT rule for vigilance classification based on spontaneous EEG activity. *Neuropsychobiology*, 17(1-2):105–17, Jan. 1987.

[147] A. Strijkstra. Subjective sleepiness correlates negatively with global alpha (8–12 Hz) and positively with central frontal theta (4–8 Hz) frequencies in the human resting awake electroencephalogram. *Neuroscience Letters*, 340(1):17–20, Apr. 2003.

[148] D. P. Subha, P. K. Joseph, R. Acharya U, and C. M. Lim. EEG Signal Analysis: A Survey. *Journal of Medical Systems*, 34(2):195–212, Dec. 2008.

[149] J. Talairach. *Co-planar stereotaxic atlas of the human brain*. 1988.

[150] C. B. Tan. The EEG and epilepsy. *Singapore medical journal*, 30(5):424–5, Oct. 1989.

[151] M. Teplan. Fundamentals of EEG measurement. *Measurement Science Review*, 2(2):1–11, 2002.

[152] K. E. Thornton and D. P. Carmody. Efficacy of traumatic brain injury rehabilitation: interventions of QEEG-guided biofeedback, computers, strategies, and medications. *Applied psychophysiology and biofeedback*, 33(2):101–24, June 2008.

[153] L. Thurstone. Attitudes can be measured. *American Journal of Sociology*, 1928.

[154] H. Tietze. Stages of fatigue during long duration driving reflected in alpha related events in the EEG. In *International Conference on Traffic and Transport Psychology*, 2000.

[155] H. Tietze. Stages of wakefulness during long duration driving reflected in alpha related events in the EEG. In *3rd International Conference on Psychophysiology in Ergonomics*, 2000.

[156] H. Tietze and V. Hargutt. Zweidimensionale Analyse zur Beurteilung des Verlaufs von Ermüdung. In *Tagung experimentell arbeitender Psychologen*, volume 49, pages 1–14, Regensburg, 2001.

[157] J. Tilmanne, J. Urbain, M. V. Kothare, A. V. Wouwer, and S. V. Kothare. Algorithms for sleep-wake identification using actigraphy: a comparative study and new results. *Journal of sleep research*, 18(1):85–98, Mar. 2009.

[158] K. L. Toh. Basic science review on circadian rhythm biology and circadian sleep disorders. *Annals of the Academy of Medicine, Singapore*, 37(8):662–8, Aug. 2008.

[159] P. Tonner and B. Bein. Classic electroencephalographic parameters: Median frequency, spectral edge frequency etc. *Best Practice & Research Clinical Anaesthesiology*, 20(1):147–159, Mar. 2006.

[160] L. Torsvall and T. Åkerstedt. Sleepiness on the job: continuously measured EEG changes in train drivers. *Electroencephalography and clinical neurophysiology*, 66(6):502–11, June 1987.

[161] USDA. Intakes of Selenium, Caffeine, and Theobromine by Adults. Technical report, 2000.

[162] W. von Ow. Praktische Anleitung zum 10-20-Elektrodensystem. *NEUROPHYSIOLOGIE LABOR*, 2002.

[163] K. Šušmáková. Classification of Waking, Sleep Onset and Deep Sleep by Single Measures. *Measurement Science Review*, 7(4):34–38, 2007.

[164] H.-G. Weess, C. Sauter, P. Geisler, W. Bohning, B. Wilhelm, M. Rotte, C. Gresele, C. Schneider, H. Schulz, R. Lund, and R. Steinberg. Vigilanz, Einschlafneigung, Daueraufmerksamkeit, Mudigkeit, Schlafrigkeit Diagnostische Instrumentarien zur Messung mudigkeits- und schlafrigkeitsbezogener Prozesse und deren Gutekriterien. Vigilance, Tendency to Fall Asleep, Sustained Attention, Tiredness. *Somnologie*, 4(1):20–38, Feb. 2000.

[165] H.-G. Weess, C. Sauter, P. Geisler, W. Bohning, B. Wilhelm, M. Rotte, C. Gresele, C. Schneider, H. Schulz, R. Lund, and R. Steinberg. Vigilanz, Einschlafneigung, Daueraufmerksamkeit, Mudigkeit, Schlafrigkeit Diagnostische Instrumentarien zur Messung mudigkeits- und schlafrigkeitsbezogener Prozesse und deren Gutekriterien. Vigilance, Tendency to Fall Asleep, Sustained Attention, Tiredness. *Somnologie*, 4(1):20–38, Feb. 2000.

[166] A. Wirz-Justice. How to measure circadian rhythms in humans. *Medicographia*, 29(1):84–90, 2007.

[167] I. World Medical Association. Declaration of Helsinki. Ethical principles for medical research involving human subjects., June 2009.

[168] N. Wright and A. McGown. Vigilance on the civil flight deck: incidence of sleepiness and sleep during long-haul flights and associated changes in physiological parameters. *Ergonomics*, 44(1):82–106, Jan. 2001.

[169] G.-Z. Yang. *Body Sensor Networks*. Springer, 2006.

[170] E. Zils. *Auswirkungen von Schlafentzug auf verschiedene Typen sakkadischer Augenbewegungen*. Thesis (phd), 2005.

[171] L. Zivin and C. A. Marsan. Incidence and prognostic significance of "epileptiform" activity in the eeg of non-epileptic subjects. *Brain : a journal of neurology*, 91(4):751–78, Jan. 1968.

I want morebooks!

Buy your books fast and straightforward online - at one of the world's fastest growing online book stores! Environmentally sound due to Print-on-Demand technologies.

Buy your books online at
www.get-morebooks.com

Kaufen Sie Ihre Bücher schnell und unkompliziert online – auf einer der am schnellsten wachsenden Buchhandelsplattformen weltweit!
Dank Print-On-Demand umwelt- und ressourcenschonend produziert.

Bücher schneller online kaufen
www.morebooks.de

OmniScriptum Marketing DEU GmbH
Heinrich-Böcking-Str. 6-8
D - 66121 Saarbrücken
Telefax: +49 681 93 81 567-9

info@omniscriptum.com
www.omniscriptum.com

Printed by Books on Demand GmbH, Norderstedt / Germany